Big Girls Do Cry

Big Girls Do Cry

MY LOVE AFFAIR WITH FRANKIE VALLI

April Kirkwood

WISE Ink
CREATIVE ★ PUBLISHING

ISBN: 978-1-940014-67-8
eISBN: 978-1-940014-84-5

Library of Congress Catalog Number: 2015945789
Printed in the United States of America
First Printing: 2015
19   18   17   16   15   5   4   3   2   1

Cover design by Nupoor Gordon
Interior design by Kim Morehead

Wise Ink Creative Publishing
Minneapolis, MN 55405
www.wiseinkpub.com

To order, visit www.itascabooks.com or call 1-800-901-3480.
Reseller discounts available.

Acknowledgments

GRACIOUS REMEMBRANCES AND THANK-YOUS

This story is dedicated to my children, Dana and Grant, for their unconditional support and love in sharing this tumultuous road with me, a life filled with laughter, dancing, drama, and so much to learn together. I am so honored that you picked me to be your mom.

> *I love you, I praise you, I appreciate you.*
> *You are God's child*
> *Great things happen to you*
> *Nothing can stop it.*

To the men mentioned in this book who have spiritually placed themselves in my physical world with some unexplainable, magnificent plan born somewhere else in the universe. Through the tears, the sorrows, and the joys, thank you for teaching me about love. You provided the right lessons I needed at the exact time I needed them. I love you all throughout eternity. I love you Daddy, Papa, Uncle Chuck, Marc, Billy, Ronnie, and, last but not least, Mr. Frankie Valli himself.

I've heard the saying that when a female loses her mother, that is the actual moment she truly grows into a woman. I'm not sure if that's correct, but I know there was a huge hole in my heart and I felt lost when I lost mine. There are a few magnificent beings who graciously stepped into her shoes and in many ways completed and corrected me in areas that only a mom could. For this, I want to publicly acknowledge Donna Simon, Margot Fontayne, Judy from Jersey, and, of course, Aunt Ginny. You have saved me in ways that can't be described but must be experienced in the heart.

Aunt Ginny, Grandma Kata, my mom, the Queen Bee herself, Beverly Jean—you are my dream team. I actually am kind of looking forward to when we will all to be together again in the heavens. You are all a huge part of the rock on which I stand.

Last of all, Miss Roxie, my teacup Yorkie who steadfastly sat with me, keeping me on task when I wanted to walk away. She endlessly supported me when all others told me to give up, that it was just another one of my whimsical fantasies. She kept me warm inside through it all, never wavering from her dedication to me and my dreams. She looked up, sighed, and slept under my feet as I typed, scribbled, giggled, shouted, sobbed, and fell silent in healing moments. If men were like you, I wouldn't have needed to write this; I would be in bliss. I love you little, I love you big, even if you were a fat little pig. You are an excellent familiar for a fairy like me!

Most importantly, *Big Girls Do Cry* goes out to all of the Mary Anns, Susans, and those who have heard the feminine call of the wolf hidden deep. Let us unite and howl, no longer isolated in the secret night. Let each she-wolf run to the top of the mountain in the bright day as we support one another to stand up and be rightfully worshipped.

I also want to extend a warm thank-you to Anthony, who passionately managed my social marketing, endlessly listened to my sob stories, and accepted my dark side. And to Dara from Wise Ink Creative Publishing; when I was disappointed, you encouraged me and were vital to bringing all of this together as a finished product. Thank you all so much. You mean more to me than words can convey.

Preface

My life has been fun, hilarious, and—at times—insane. Your life has probably been that way too. At other moments I managed to thrive more above the clouds where fairies dance with birds and sleep in the tails of squirrels under the moon. Let's face it: dysfunctional is the new normal. We could probably sit down at a coffee shop somewhere in the United States and share stories that would make each other laugh or cry and maybe sometimes both.

This book is full of stories about my life and the important people in it. I see myself with the heart of Marilyn Monroe raised by a mom like from the famous play, *Gypsy Rose Lee*. Between these pages are those who most affected the best and worst of the highs and lows. There's my personal dream team (my mother, Aunt Ginny, and Grandma), my children (Dana and Grant), my husbands (Marc and Billy), my current love (Ron), and the guy on the cover, Frankie Valli. You know who he is, right? A little guy from Nutley, New Jersey, raised in the projects, his dad a barber and his mom the heart of the home.

He was born Francesco Stephen Castelluccio on May 3, 1934, with a voice of gold. He lived life large, surviving all his ups and downs, still going strong like the ever-ready Energizer bunny he compares himself to. Frankie Valli has millions of adoring fans who still hold him close to their hearts and connect his music with stories of their own lives.

Mothers have the most profound effect on us. Even today, years after her passing, I wonder, am I following in my mother's footsteps, deathly afraid of change and abandonment? Perhaps that's one possible explanation to why I held on to the wish that Frankie Valli would take me far away into a romantic fantasy, escaping my mother's violent, temperamental, unstable way of life. Her world was filled with post-Depression economic hardships and abuse. Still, humans instinctively struggle to survive, even in the most obscene ways. Beverly found her way over the rainbow by swallowing any medication in sight, displacing her dreary, lackluster reality with a world of dreams where her heart would never be broken. The lives of each of us are about this serious shit, the blood and guts we don't want to see and most definitely don't want to speak of. This is the core of our discontent and our self-loathing. We hate ourselves for lacking the courage to seek the moon and the stars. Instead, we settle for a crappy job, a lousy marriage, disrespectful kids, and boring sermons at church that answer nothing. But that's not the face we present to the rest of the world. We laugh, turning up the music and dancing as if we were perfectly cool, keeping all the balls in the air like a star in some pathetic carnival show. In truth, all we are juggling is our own self-deception, telling ourselves that we have cunningly manipulated the perception others have of us. It's sick, it's sad, and it's killing us all from the inside out. But for me and, I suspect, many other lovers who are cornered in their own despair, this is a slow death leading us to living in isolation and confusion, leaving us mortally wounded and incapable of moving either forward or backward. Imprinting: it's not in the psychological bible of diagnosis, *The Diagnostic and Statistical Manual of Mental Disorders*, fifth edition (or DSM-5), but maybe it should be. Well, let me tell you, if I could have fixed that issue in just the clients, family members, and friends I know, I believe there would be millions more who wouldn't need continual nonproductive psychotropic therapy, counseling, and support groups, because they have been mistakenly labeled with a Band-Aid diagnosis, such as "situational depression" or "adjustment disorder." The theory that whatever we resist will persist is evident in our divorce rate. Just to throw in a carrot, isn't it nice to know not everything is Mommy's or Daddy's fault? We give them way too much power anyway. Now the child in us might just need to become accountable for some of our biggest adult mishaps.

While you read about the traumatic events that I experienced on my grandmother's chicken farm, you'll also learn about the long-lasting effects that still linger in my being today. Yes, little April is alive and well.

The lessons from those events compounded in ways I would have never believed, from the moment I first saw Frankie at the tender age of six, throughout my teenage years and into my adulthood. It was only recently that I learned how my personal imprint dictated every major decision regarding relationships in my life.

I didn't make the best choices throughout my life. I'm optimistic that after reading this book, you can make better decisions that will ensure a long life of happiness with the perfect fit for you. Even designer shoes hurt if the size is wrong and—still more upsetting—when the size is right.

So sit back, read, laugh, cry, and—hopefully—learn.

CHAPTER 1

Fallen Angel

The first time I saw him, I loved him. He had me at "Sherry." He had me at "Opus 17." He had me at "Tell It to the Rain." I didn't know the songs, but I knew him from somewhere. My family didn't love the music; they went for me. The first time I heard the music I was barely six. Even as a young girl, I remember the odd feelings that filled up the innermost part of my being.

My family was made of strong-willed women who never took "no" for an answer. I was bred to bring home victory much like Seabiscuit, the little horse who shocked the entire world. My family's keen marketing strategy for their little filly was a winner, and I got Frankie's attention. I got invited backstage after a show one night with my aunt Ginny and Grandma. After that, each time it was as though we were automatically given backstage passes. I began to know the song order, and I would start to cry on cue when they sang "Let's Hang On." I knew there was only one song left before it was over. Frankie would pick me up and carry me around like a proud father with his baby girl. I loved the attention. I'd smile at the people. I'd nuzzle his neck.

The mystery of it all is that it made absolutely no logical sense how it came to be—it was destiny. I come from humble beginnings and a Pentecostal upbringing. I come from no Italian Mafia ties nor did I know anyone in Jersey or New York.

Soon, whenever Frankie and the other guys in the band were in the Ohio area, it was natural for them to see my special hat and know the "little girl" was only steps behind, waiting for permission to visit. It was my calling card, my assurance he would remember me and let me backstage. I usually sent it before the concert. A tip for groupies: go early when sound check is about to happen.

Oh, I had a few crushes during all this Frankie Valli madness. In middle school, there was Peter: tall, lanky, manically biting his nails, playing all sorts of flirtatious games with me. He had the most brilliant brown eyes that sparkled when he spoke, full of every kind of mischief possible. Whether it was always picking me last in kickball or putting my sunbonnet in the tree on the last day of school, Peter had this enchanting way of getting my attention. I think that energy must have gotten him into trouble, smoking too much pot and creating chaos for his very educated and respectable parents, who sent him away to a military school of sorts to straighten him out. After that he became a childhood memory. He followed his dream for a while, training in Europe and New York to be an opera singer. I still wonder what truly became of him. But he was never Frankie, although he looked and acted like my first crush at times. He was the first bad boy who caught my eye.

The good boy, David, was truly a great guy, the one I should have kept but let go. He was a typical Midwestern kid with blond hair and hazel eyes, short and husky. He's the one I should have married, the one I went to church with. We would have gone to Oral Roberts together, but he slipped through my fingers. There were moments when I knew what love was because of David. He sent me flowers at school, and when he went skiing or to Florida, I always got the most charming cards with messages of adoration. I never responded the way I should have. I lost out. I have no idea where he is, but I wish I would have taken his space and his genuine feelings more respectfully.

In high school, I was already shut down in so many ways. I was on fast-forward within the confines of appropriate behavior. I dated my aunt Ginny's second husband's brother, Dale Crain. He was older than me, but of course with Aunt Ginny and Uncle Bill I was always looked after. Whether it was my mom fist-fighting in the yard or girls being mean to me at a bar, my aunt to this day is my safe place. And I was socially such a late bloomer. Going to a high school party scared the shit out of me. Besides, there were modeling classes, baton lessons, pageants, and studying that took up most of my waking hours. I wouldn't think of disobeying my mom, as she was so fragile. Children have a deep knowing of when they need to be on task. I was here to keep my mom level, or at least I tried to be. Dale was blond with blue eyes, and he treated me like a princess. Every Sunday we would take long rides into the countryside and talk and talk. One Christmas a huge brightly wrapped gift was brought in but the gift wasn't there. I opened it, digging to the bottom through tissues papers only to find on the bottom of the box a poem written and colored into the shape of a wreath:

I said it was big,
but it's not in this box,
it must be just right,
for you, little fox.
Could it be a dog,

a camera,
or a locket?

Well, look and you'll see,
It's in my right pocket.

Dale continued his loving gestures on Easter arriving in one of his souped-up cars. Dale loved his cars and spent most of his night's tinkering in the garage, a safe haven for him, I suppose, from his journey to Vietnam and back. On the passenger's side sat adorable giant Raggedy Ann and Andy dolls, perfume, and a Seals and Crofts album. When I became Miss Ohio Teenager in Columbus, Ohio, he was there, cheering me on as giant crocodile tears poured down his face, clapping with wild abandon. When I won the title, I looked down, and he stood at the bottom of the stage just like Prince Charming, handing me a bouquet of red roses and giving me a gentle kiss on the cheek. Of course, the day was a bit dampened when my stepfather almost pushed my mother out of the skyscraper hotel. But like the star child I was, I went on that stage and made everyone proud, for we all know the show must go on.

I realized, like a young dragonfly stumbling to fly out of the murky waters into the sky, that my soul's voice was urging me to go on and experience new adventures as well. I see a trend now, looking back: men always wanted to keep me in their private fish bowl. If I stay, I will grow only to the size they permit. I want to grow, and sometimes that means going away or jumping out and lying on the floor, gasping for air until the spirit scoops me up and places me in a larger pool. I wanted to jump into a bigger pond even if I found that pond to be smaller than the one I came from.

It was my junior year of high school, and I felt the choking clench of youth around my neck each time Dale phoned faithfully each morning waking me up and each night before I went to bed. He was a perfect boyfriend, but I saw my life shortened in experiences slipping into a life being a young bride. I was a filly and I wanted to jump the fence and break free into the unknown. I shared these thoughts with my mom. She spoke as a master of the heart, "Just break up a little in your mind each day." I glanced over at her like a typical teenager who just received the most ridiculous advice ever from none other than a mom. She continued in her authoritative manner, not glancing at my crinkled-up nose and rolling eyes and continued. "Then, one morning, April Lynn, you'll get up and know it's over for you. There's no need to rush. It takes months sometimes. One morning you will open your eyes and your heart will be free and you will know it's the day to say goodbye." I tried it. It took me six months, but good gracious, it actually worked. I'm always amazed and dazed how my mother was so wise in so many ways and so clueless in others. Maybe we are all like that. We come into this world with a certain knowing of things and blind as a bat to other issues yet to be learned. One morning, the sun rose, and I stretched from a dreamy, peaceful rest, had a cup of tea, and then went to my princess phone near my white, lacy canopy bed to sit a moment. Then, without so much as a second of hesitation, I coldly broke it off with Dale over the phone. I thought to myself, My mom just might know what she's talking about once in a while.

However, I don't always give so much attention to what I'm about to do. I've made some mistakes. I just kind of fly by the seat of my pants, and the cost of those flights can be more expensive than True Religion jeans. But with Dale, I did it right. I respected him and broke it off before I went to see Frankie, and then I met Mark. Just recently at his brother's funeral, my uncle Bill, who was once married to my aunt

Ginny, told me that there were photos of Dale and me together in Florida. He was another nice guy I let go for my Jersey Boy.

Spring is so magnificent in the Midwest. I'm sure that's where Walt Disney got his picturesque scenes for those romantic animated movies. Fragrant blossoms covered the trees in shades of pink and purple and new grass sprouted on every lawn along the drive from my house to Stambaugh Auditorium, leading me back to that familiar place where I also attended church and the Kathryn Kuhlman Ministry for so many years. For some, love may have been in the air, but that wasn't on my agenda. I just wanted to see my friend, one of the most-celebrated artists in the history of music. A friend whom I looked up to, admired. He had it all going on— Italian, gold chains, Vegas attitude, all the stuff that made women swoon back then and, in some cases, still does today. Power is still one of the sexiest aphrodisiacs.

As a six-year-old, you think of an old man like a dad. Frankie was the perfect dad. With him, all my dreams came true. I imagine now that he rather liked that I followed behind him like his little shadow. Perhaps I reminded him of one of his little girls. His daughter Toni is very attractive, with blond hair, and I can see how there might have been a resemblance of her in my eyes. I didn't know that then. I didn't know that he reminded me of my dad back then either. We obviously found something in one another that sparked a connection.

After I parked my used, little, dull, gold-colored Chevy in the parking lot, I headed to the backstage entrance while others walked up the huge marble steps, past the Corinthian columns, and through the front doors. I proceeded to sneak backstage as though I were on a spy mission to find the king. All of a sudden, he was standing there in the flesh, staring at me from head to toe.

"You're all grown up," he said.

I gulped, blushed, and somehow managed to utter in a

small voice, "Do you know who I am?"

He grinned with a boyish charm. "Yes, September."

I was stunned and flattered. All grown up, Miss Ohio Teenager, charm schools, pageants, and now he knew me. I was impressed at him and at myself. Yes, September is just what he called me, which told me he remembered my name in a sexy and playful way. I love men who play. Role-play, joke play, and whatever else makes me giggle with a slight hand of deception, and I'm theirs.

At that moment, I was transformed from a little girl to a woman. I arrived with the thoughts of a child, but with one simple touch of his hand brushing up against my skin it was as though lightning struck my being, infusing me with strange feelings I had never felt before. When I arrived that early spring evening and parked my car behind the giant stone building filled with so many magical moments from my childhood, I was just there to see my friend, someone I looked forward to seeing whenever he came to Youngstown. But as with all beginnings, electricity filled the room and everything else faded into a fog.

Frankie stood little in stature but with a powerful presence, the kind of charisma you have to be born with. His dark black eyes penetrated my beige lace top, the few gold chains tangled around my neck, and my long hair lying on my chest. He kissed me on the forehead and marveled at my beauty, then did the most erotic thing any man has ever done. He was perfectly still. He walked ever so close to my chest. Tenderly he untangled my gold chains. It felt like a million moments waiting with each movement, and I hoped he wouldn't feel my heart pounding inside my chest. Blood gushed into previously dormant areas of my body, awakening them for the first time. The room whirled around him, as did I. When he touched me, I became delirious, and my stomach jumped. For a moment, I lost all feeling, like I was floating on the proverbial cloud of ecstasy. I was addicted to him and the surge and rush I felt near him. My soul bounced back into my body when someone knocked on the dressing room door. When they left, Frankie asked if I wanted to come backstage after the show. I think I said yes, trying to act cool and collected. But I probably could only nod, as I'm sure no sound would come out of my mouth; he had stolen my wind.

I began to rationalize what I was about to do. Why wouldn't I go to see Frankie Valli at his hotel? I'd been going backstage for years. Why should tonight be any different? But it was. He knew it, and so did I.

CHAPTER 2

In My Mother's Eyes

I was born the same time Barbie arrived on the scene. Every female under the age of twelve gazed at Barbie's perfection, hearing the message, "This is what a beautiful woman looks like." She had it all—height, boobs, clothes, a cool car, a poodle, a best friend Madge, and most of all, Ken. Barbie's image created a generation of women with self-esteem issues before they hit their first high school dance. It was also a period in history when society gave women freedoms never experienced before. April Lynn Gatta, born December 3, 1957, to Beverly Jean and Ralph Gatta, was born into an age where television spoon fed our desires. On a personal level, the marriage of Beverly and Ralph Gatta was typical of the sixties rebellion and social confusion. A union made more in hell than heaven; at least in accordance with staunch Pentecostal values from the late '50s, when Catholics and Protestants were not permitted to intermarry. Worse yet, the very thought of an Anglo-Saxon marrying an Italian was a faux pas. It was before birth control and a time when you found out if you were pregnant only if the rabbit died. One bathroom, one phone, and a coal cellar to keep the house heated in the winters. My grandmother wore black to the wedding, openly protesting, as the liberal pioneer she was, against the unholy ceremony joining my mom and my dad as husband and wife. The Italian side of my dad's family created a wedding that was one of the largest events at that time with cookies, champagne, and music overflowing from morning til night. I was born nine months later.

Youngstown, Ohio, is nestled between Pittsburgh and Cleveland. This quiet city became better known as Bomb Town, USA, for its Mafia wars and syndicated crime affiliations. More cars were bombed in that city than anywhere else in the country. It was also a growing steel-mill metropolis, which meant money was flowing for all classes of people. This flagrant excess called a need for the darkest of pool halls, beer gardens, and cathouses. It was a melting pot of uneducated immigrants in little neighborhoods of segregated Italians, Poles, and Greeks. For the first time in American history, the middle class grew strong, with incomes comparable to successful white-collar workers. However, my young life nestled amid the fields of a simple chicken farm was oblivious to all that was dark and sinister.

My days were more concerned with watching how tall corn stalks grew and how to care for baby kitties. With only three stations on television, I had more to do outside in the chicken coops or my playhouse. On Sundays the entire town was closed to attend church. We always went to church, always. We were there for Christ Crusades, revival meetings, and summer Sunday school camp. Throughout the years we attended the First Assembly of God, the Pleasant Valley Evangelical Church, and the Kathryn Kuhlman Ministry held at Stambaugh Auditorium. It didn't matter, because nothing was open on Sundays anyway, not even a small corner store to pick up milk for lunch.

But on Saturdays, whether it was in a gorgeous house in the city or a simple farmhouse with a tire swing and a lazy dog sitting under a willow tree, teenagers synchronously tuned in to *American Bandstand* and tapped their toes to dirty dancing, teased hair, and popping chewing gum. Yes, it was a new time of experimentation and self-expression.

For me though, Fridays were always one of my favorite days. I would go with Grandma to deliver eggs to the maids and well-dressed wives with red nails and high heels. I remember one house that had these soft, crimson velvet chairs in the foyer where I was allowed to sit and suck my thumb.

Who would have known that I, a little peanut, as called by my aunt Gigi, had the same astrological first house as none other than sex kitten Miss Marilyn Monroe herself. It was as though I was predestined to be born in an era that gave little girls from nowhere a chance to change their lives and follow their dreams. I was petite, with big brown eyes that could steal gold from the homeless with a simple smile and twirl of my dress, a valuable skill enabling me to run the race with the best of them. With the adoration and attention given to all firstborn babies, my dream team gave me the magic wand to believe that dreams can come true and anything is possible with God on my side.

I was raised by three fiercely strong women whom O. J. Simpson would have wanted for his defense team—my mother, grandmother, and Aunt Ginny, a.k.a. my dream team. Our home was filled with Pentecostal hymns, depression, dancing in the kitchen, and struggles to define the new female role in a liberal world. Burn the bra, bring the Bible, add a bit of the bubbly—this was the beginning of a new era with no guidelines. It was a time of making up the rules as you go, and I was tiptoeing ever so lightly behind them, watching and mimicking their every step.

My grandmother was the original liberated woman, writing her own rules and overcoming the odds the best she knew how with the tools she had to work with. I remember speaking at her funeral recounting that my grandma shared the same birthdate of that famous outspoken sex symbol, Mae West. To this day, each time I visit a medium she floats in and they describe her as the curvy woman who always wore a dress and high heels. That was my grandma, my mentor, my strength. I was told that she was once the lady that could out drink and outparty anyone in Youngstown, Ohio. During WWII she worked in a factory. She also shared with me throughout many intimate conversations the hardship of single-handedly digging her own basement while nine months pregnant with my aunt Larene. Larene, by the way, was named by Grandma's husband as he sauntered in with her on one arm and a bottle of whiskey on the other. There were whispers of hanger abortions, walking to the dentist in snowstorms, and cleaning homes for the rich for her survival. Virginia Mae Ohl Kata is still the matriarch and cornerstone of the devotion I feel when I think of my childhood. After being given a few acres in the woods in the middle of Ohio by her biological mother, referred to only as Aunt Marie, my grandmother became one of the first stay-at-home female business owners, long before it was hip and trendy. She owned a few thousand chickens and did financially well. She was a strong-willed woman who raised six children from three different men. An unwed mother, she walked miles in the snow during her teen years to work so she could pay for her son in an orphanage. No one offered to buy her a car for her unselfish service to her little boy. No one cared. She was married two times and was a product of the Great Depression, where fear won the blue ribbon as primary motivator and security the runner-up for most of the decisions she made.

We saved everything. I mean everything! She would wear panty hose with knots tied in the toes where there were snags and tears. In our basement, near the coal furnace, were shelves holding every sort of item: plastic bags, rubber bands, string, wick, panty hose, jars, boxes, plastic containers, and more. We were waiting for the second coming of Christ as implied by the Book of Revelation from the King James Version of the Bible. Billy Graham told us, Jimmy Swaggart sang about it, and so we believed it.

But it wasn't just demographics that turned Virginia Mae Ohl Kata into such a fierce survivor. The young woman knew nothing of love and safety. She suffered from severe neglect as an orphan herself. As a newborn, her head was misshapen because Aunt Marie tied her corset so tight to hide her protruding baby bump. She was passed from caregiver to caregiver for many years to save her biological mother's teaching position, which was coveted in society back then. So she ran away early, packing only her scars of abuse and incest in search for something more. She carried with her the kind of pain and sorrow that creates a deep, agonizing desire to find some refuge from not being wanted, as well as a burning rage to rebel and challenge everyone she knew.

Over years of secrets and stories, my grandmother recounted the most important point in her simple existence: "Having enough of this old world, I bought a one-way ticket to get on a train, because I was going to throw myself off. I was standing on the caboose, gazing down onto the tracks, ready to leap, when out of nowhere I heard a small voice saying, 'Virginia, I love you. You are my child. You are safe.'" I still recall the warm glow on her face as she quietly recounted this moment, so dignified, sitting and sipping instant Maxwell House coffee in the kitchen while the white organdy drapes cast a soft shadow protecting her eyes from the sun. It was as though the wind was blowing in celebration. "I felt God's presence for the first time, and I dedicated the rest of my life to knowing him and walking in his path." Grandma and I enjoyed many conversations like that.

She was there when I went into labor with Dana, when everyone else was at work, and kept feeding me spaghetti because she said the labor would be long and would take hours. Well, that wasn't exactly the case. Baby Dana was transverse, and since I ate so much, I had to stay awake. Grandma felt awful. I was scared to death, but with fourteen family members pouring into the same hospital where we were all born, that little girl came out fine.

Grammy, president of my dream team, was there through it all, teaching me everything from how to clean the floors or the steps to holding a profitable garage sale. She was there to discuss all the secrets women yearn to share with one another, and when I'm cleaning under the kitchen sink, I often feel her presence. Love never dies, does it?

Speaking of passion, her last husband, John Kata, known as Bumpy to us kids, was a handsome city slicker with a zest for women and card playing who married Grandma under a false name to avoid being deported. We never knew when their real anniversary was, and every year Grandma was hurt to say the least. Their marriage had its ups and downs, but nothing so damaging as when Grandma gave her life to the Lord. Sorry to say, he didn't appreciate or understand the new Virginia. As the years went by, their onetime hot-and-heavy marital intimacy was slowly replaced with stale conversations focusing on children, their garden, and the weather. Every Saturday night, Bumpy went out to play cards and Grandma got ready to teach Sunday school. Why is it that life changes and others can't see the beauty in it but instead dig in their heels, bury their heads in the sand, and resist? Still, there was an old-fashioned respect for our quiet Bumpy. When he did speak, we listened, and he insisted we always respect Grandma no matter what. After he passed, my grandma fell apart, and I moved in with Dana and Grant until she got too bad. Mom took Grandma and sent her to church day care. Years later, in 2006, Grandma passed away at home at ninety-one years young on Thanksgiving morning.

My mother, Beverly Jean, Grandma's first daughter, born May 3, 1937, had an aristocratic aura with a Princess Grace appeal rather than that of a poor girl from a chicken farm. She had white skin like a pearl, auburn hair, and eyes of hazel that would burn a hole in your heart if she were angry. She only had to give us one glaring stare to cause my brother and me to stop whatever we were doing and wait for her wrath. She had that kind of power. One person she couldn't control was herself. Somewhere in her mind, things were never quite right. Before Oprah, Dr. Phil, and mainstream counseling, girls like Beverly were just viewed as trouble.

She would scream bloody murder in first grade until she was removed, desk and all. One of her favorite rituals was to sit up in the tree at our local cemetery, listening to funeral rites, then bring the flowers home to put in her bedroom, a small room that she shared with four others. On hot summer days when everyone was seeking shade under a tree or swinging from vines in the woods, she would yell to planes, begging them to come down and take her away. This was an actor in the making. She married my father, Ralph Gatta, because she never received any word from the love of her life who was away at college. While Ralph was a quiet, elegant, softly spoken man with a desire to play music and live quietly, Miss Beverly Jean was full of laughter with flashing eyes and wishes for adventure. Unfortunately for everyone, my grandma hid letters from my mom's true love. Rebound and revenge is dangerous and deadly. Today, I realize my mom suffered her entire life, looking in all the wrong places for solace and help. The only help she ever got was by self-medicating with prescription pills and brief affairs with her doctors and bosses. As much as I tried, I was never enough for her. I couldn't be nor should I have been expected to be the one who made her life complete. That is an inside job.

I can't emphasize more emphatically: she was once beautiful, vivacious, and quite an interesting character, full of passion and energy. People—well, men especially—were naturally drawn to her vitality. I think I inherited that from her. Even as distraught and self-destructive as she was, there were moments when she was insightful beyond measure and loved me more than life itself. Her life was a mixture of pain and passion, with a desire to escape both. Her demise was her own. But perhaps that is the truth for each of us, in less dramatic terms. Either way, the pain that troubled her all her life led me and my siblings down a path of instability and confusion when we looked for the parental guidance and support that every child needs and deserves.

My mother, the Queen Bee, as she was most appropriately called, wanted only the best for me, but not just like devoted mothers do. She was driven to make her life worthwhile through my existence. Her dedication to seeing me do more than well in life could mask the cloud that overshadowed even her most successful attempts to bring joy into her own days. Needless to say, I am indebted because this is the kind of commitment that offered me the many opportunities to reach my potential: beauty pageants, elegant clothes, plane rides (which were a luxury back then), and college (which was not common for women from the middle class). As a child, I would catch her sobbing into a washcloth, sitting at the kitchen table after another fight with my stepfather. Seeing me step into the light, she would try to gain composure, but I felt her sorrow. I always did. It taught me lessons not many children know. Life is hard. You cry. You keep going. You keep trying.

Just like the famous Broadway mother in Gypsy Rose Lee, the Queen Bee would joke about the purple cow that would visit her bed and tell her of costumes, dances, and speeches for me to win beauty pageants with. I was being groomed to be something for as long as I can remember, though what is still quite unclear to me. Seriously, I owned more than thirty-five pairs of shoes when I was only four years of age. I attended twirling classes, jazz classes, charm classes, and modeling schools. And it seemed that I won every contest I entered. Each night after school, I walked with a book on my head, practiced baton, or went to church. It was a busy life filled with goals set in motion at my birth or maybe even before in some cosmic life plan written in the Akashic Records.

Many people feel that only trashy people put their daughters in pageants. I think it's more that women who never accomplished their own dreams push their baby birds to fly any way they can. If you graduated from Harvard and are married to a heart surgeon, you want that for your child. If you work in a dirty factory, with no college education, you figure out any way out and up—if the moment didn't arrive for themselves, they were going to make sure it happened for their kids. There is a caste system in America on some level. It's possible to move up the ladder, but not with the true blue bloods of Camelot in America. This is a cautionary tale for all aspiring starlets and actors who have been pushed by their parents. Somehow the lines get blurred, and our personal desires and theirs get all smashed together in one single dressing room. My mother loved me so much and hated her life even more, so she lost sight of where the line of healthy boundaries was. Between her lousy factory job, her unsatisfying marriage, and her disappointment in religion, I can see how it went this far.

At first it was one small pageant at the Eastwood Mall, where I placed in the top five. Then it grew into classes, walking, talking, speech-making, and dancing. My mother created a young lady willing to please at any cost. I still find myself lost in that role. I guess I still haven't given up that childlike belief of finding the best in humanity. Each morning I brush my hair into a ponytail with a red ribbon and close my eyes to yesterday with the hope that my "Eveready Bunny" perseverance will earn respect by the right people, a.k.a. the nice people, not necessarily the popular or rich people.

While I was active in the pageant scene, my classmates giggled and had a blast tiptoeing into their basements for make-out parties and beer. High school became so lonely for me. I had no friends. No one liked me. With each title, my world became smaller. Oh yeah, teachers liked me, but you can't hang out with teachers. It was so awkward. I think that's why I wanted to be a guidance counselor. I wanted to nourish those who weren't invited to the parties or picked for homecoming court. The ones whom everyone rolled their eyes at when they walked down the halls. The silent glances. Two very vicious majorettes put my bra on the church steeple at band camp. The entire band had to come to the eating area and stir until someone fessed up. I don't remember much of what happened after that except feeling embarrassed and wanting to go home.

My one true friend, Aunt Ginny, made my life not just bearable, but fun, even in just hanging around. In the end, she is the one who saved me from jealous girls, shy boys, and family who hated both of us for our bond. She rubbed my feet when I couldn't walk alone. She watched me make mistakes. When I turned away from her, I always came back. Without her I would have been a social outcast and a loner. She brings my light back when it is almost out, when I call crying for a way out. My mom, my grandma, and my aunt Ginny are actually the wind that carries me even now when Mom and Gram are in heaven. I feel them, can sense them, hear their words, and appreciate my aunt so much more than I ever told them. They are the workers, and I am just their little girl.

Eventually, the pressure on me to perform for my mother and my desire to please above all else drained me of the joy of just being a teenager. I became confused and agitated. I wasn't sure if this was something I truly desired. Was it all for her? Was it for me? It became a miserable hobby. After a near breakdown, I was given a little shih tzu that I called Lovebug, and I instantly fell in love with her. She was my friend, my confidante, my buddy. After I won Miss Ohio Teenager in 1975, I left the pageant scene because of my height. This was a decade in both the fashion and entertainment business when height wasn't just desirable, but necessary. You couldn't be an airline stewardess unless you were five foot four and weighed within their specifications. I was five foot two.

Looking back, I'm proud of my accomplishments and very grateful for all my mother did for me, or her, or both of us. She said on her deathbed, "Someone had to pay the price. I don't regret one thing I did for you, April Lynn," as I painted her toes for the last time our favorite color, that classic, lady-like Revlon Red. During the final days at the hospital as she took her last breaths, not sure if she was truly ready to say goodbye, the Queen Bee took charge, died, came back, and stayed alert to the last second. She also managed to somehow arrange for the world to see April Lynn in a new light.

I watched in amazement the strength and stamina this woman had. It was amazing to see her body blow up, shrink, get hot, and get cold, her eyes wide awake, never taking her gaze off us. When the priest was called in for last rites by my aunt and uncle (we weren't Catholic), as I was told later, Beverly Jean looked very similar to his sister who passed only a while ago. He stood still, frozen, with all my family waiting in a circle for prayer. I got a pillow and lay oh-so-close to my mother on my knees and began to pray, chant, sing, as spirit guided, reciting words and verses I didn't even remember. She did it again. She called me to stand up and be seen, not this time as a beauty queen, but as a child of God. The lines were definitely blurred between her and me. She was cool and warm, giving and envious, loving and resentful, making me feel like a failure never able to please but always wanting to. All I know now is that people see me on the street and tell me stories about how I was the center of Beverly Jean's world. I miss that crazy, contemptuous creature who created me, wanting now as an adult to get her help, send her to rehab, and then to Florida to have the life she wanted but gave to me instead.

I keep a picture of my mother's work shoes as a reminder that all I am or have is in part because of her sacrifice. As she indignantly planned her ending by not eating, rejecting transfusions, asking me if I got paid, saying goodbye to neighbors, punching ambulance drivers, demanding she stay home, knowing they would revive her, I saw the powerhouse of this lady, and it went far beyond death. We had promised each other she would stay with me. When I returned to work the following week, my principal changed the room where I taught counseling classes. I opened one of the doors to find a shelf of books. On the top of the stack was a book that somehow called to me. It was titled *Time To Go*. It was a story about a boy leaving and promising that he would return. I brought it home to share with my aunt. The next morning she called to me asking if I had seen the cover. I thought, of course, but I gazed down and found something of a miracle. The book was written by a woman with the first name Beverly and illustrated by a man with the first name Thomas. It was printed in a way to read, Beverly Thomas—my mom's name. That wasn't the only time she made her presence felt. Mom has appeared to us on several occasions in dreams calling us on the phone sending hints and cues that only certain people would know. Lights have flickered, pictures have dropped; oh yeah, Queen Bee is still around.

As an adult, I've worked through the anger. I see now that she was mentally ill—perhaps with borderline personality disorder or worse—antisocial, and doing the best she could with what she had. Isner or worse that she was mentally

I was voted "Best Dressed" and "Best Body" in high school, though I was a late bloomer and afraid to use the bathroom because girls were mean and vicious to me and I hated to have my clothes smell of smoke. I know I was the goody two-shoes everyone hated. I got that message clearly when I found a dead fish in my locker, when a group of girls beat me up and left me in Liberty Plaza, and when others threw stones at me as I marched down the field. Later, my stepfather and I got into a fight, and he threw my fire batons in the field. Such is my life. I keep swimming. Finally, my principal, Mr. Grant Dieter, and my band director, Mr. Purser, met with me and gave me permission to protect myself. But no matter what adults told me to do to defend myself, I couldn't fight; I didn't know how. It just wasn't in my DNA. Even today in our gated community in South Florida, a woman said to me, "Oh, the ladies won't like you. You're too attractive." Why are girls so mean? Anyway, Mom always assured me in a stoic voice when similar social scenes like these hurt my feelings, "If someone's not jealous when you walk into a room, you've lost your edge." I've learned that's not exactly true, but I get what she was trying to say.

Virginia Lee Wieland, key BFF of the dream team, was only eleven years old when I was born. She was the cool big sister every girl dreams of. Tall, blond, crystal-blue eyes, the total opposite of me. And wow was she smart. She could have been or done anything. She was held back only by her own self-doubts. Ginny, a Gemini, is sensitive in nature, protected only by that mouth of hers. She is like a plain brown paper bag; you have to risk putting your hand in to find out what's inside. Is it a pile of poop or diamonds? I found jewels inside that bag of hers; others have missed out. What she offers is worth more than money. When my cousin Kathy died at thirty-two from cancer, my aunt defended me when even then, on her deathbed, Kathy made some catty remarks about me. Now that's love, as both of us girls were her nieces and she loved Kathy, as do I. As the years went by, I dated the brother of her first husband. We scheduled surgeries together. When I was little, everyone thought I was her daughter. It's always been that way. She never left my side when my mother was passing. Aunt Ginny is the only member left of my dream team, a daunting task for any one person.

In retrospect, I think they must have known. My mother asked if I wanted to be on birth control pills. I said yes. We drove to the doctor's office and never uttered another word about it. Ten years earlier, I might have been the mother of Frankie Valli's children. The generation I grew up in determined many different outcomes for my life completely unique to our age group. It's a fascinating study to imagine being born into a different time or a different city. My mom was so private. For all that we talked, we never talked about the important shit: how to pick a great husband, how to survive in the world, and how to be decent without going bat-shit nutty.

So it's true, my dream team was instrumental in meeting Frankie Valli. I know as sure as I'm writing this that they had only the best of intentions. I certainly don't believe they ever meant to hurt me. I loved Frankie Valli so much they must have thought about what they could do to help get me close to him, even at a prepubescent age. So it began very innocently. Many things that others judge us for all start off that way, don't you agree?

Back then, our generation believed true love lasted forever. The Disney movies tell us so. Prince Charming finds the slipper and marries us, and we ride off in his Porsche. However, we have now discovered, often the hard way, that it doesn't happen the way we thought. I wonder if Sleeping Beauty would have rather stayed asleep!

And whose fault is it that our lives become a romantic mishmash resembling a tragedy more than a romance? Mommy, Daddy, or you? Think back for a moment about all the important love interests in your life. You automatically spit out the names of your present spouse or companion. Those are the people in your life right now. Are you truly in love with them? If not, why? What is it you are looking for in a partner? Is it even real? Would you want it if you had it?

I have disappointed many men who wanted eye candy and then found out I wear a ponytail and dash about in overalls most of the time; save newborn bunnies, put them in the laundry room, and feed them with a dropper; and put my kids first. Just work with me here; part of your romantic problems might be a result of something else. Is it you who distances yourself from that special someone who gives their love to you? Are you exaggerating over little assaults on your ego, making a mountain out of a molehill so you have reason to pull back, recoil, and shut the door to your heart? Is forgetting to pull the car in the garage at night a sin? Is spending too much at the hair salon reason to fight? Are nights out with the guys at the bar reason to throw a tantrum? Maybe you even resent their commitment to their career because you feel slighted. Seriously, as years go by, we calculate one grievance heaped upon another so that we deceive ourselves into thinking we are just in going out and hunting for someone new. When we start this kind of merry-go-round, we become chronic losers in finding the one. Maybe it's because we mislabel what real love is from the beginning.

CHAPTER 3

Can't Take My Eyes Off of You

So where was I?

Before I left to take my seat near the stage, I thought, I'm going to marry Frankie Valli. So for the first time, I looked at him in a different light while he sang all those hits we love: "Sherry," "Big Girls Don't Cry," "Walk Like a Man," "Candy Girl," and "Ain't That a Shame." I looked at him as my future husband. I didn't know at the time that he was married to a beautiful blond by the name of Mary Ann, who, by the way, is on the cover of one of his albums. To be honest, I don't think it would have mattered. The man I wanted as my husband stood on that stage and wooed the audience with a voice that I now considered dreamy, seductive, and sexy.

After the show, I went backstage and waited for him to take off his makeup, shower, and change clothes. Of course, there were radio folks to meet, a crowd that knew him, and a little PR from the press. Back then, interviews were done on location. It was so interesting to watch and be a small part of. He would smile and wink across the room as he answered their questions, edging himself nearer to me. Then he whispered in my ear, "Let's go for a drink at my hotel. It's the Holiday Inn on Belmont Avenue. Do you know where it is? Did you drive here?" Even being underage, I couldn't say no to my future spouse. The hotel was located midway between the auditorium and my house, not far from my high school. Little did I ever dream that I would end up in his room at this Holiday Inn that I had driven past so many times as I went to shop with my family at the Liberty Plaza. Now, not only was I there with the actual Frankie Valli, but I was totally alone with him not knowing what to say or how to act.

He kissed me on my neck and then up my face and on my eyes. Of course, my knees got weak, and I shivered while my insides melted. Here I was, in a hotel room, with Frankie Valli. Kissing him. Life couldn't have been better. When he asked if I wanted to be with him, I replied with as much confidence as I could muster, "Uh-huh." Life just got a lot better. All my dreams were coming true. No more Barbie and Frankie dolls role-playing what our life would be like. It was really us in real life. At least that's how it seemed.

Truth be told, I didn't know what I was doing. I'd never done this before. He had to direct me, like a lover should with someone new. My body tingled. The galloping horse ran a few laps more around the inside of my chest. I savored his touch. His kisses. His hair. His voice. I even adored how he always put french fries on his hamburger.

He was thirty-nine and absolutely stunning in every way. He walked around naked in the hotel room. I just lay there in bed, shocked by his boldness. We finished much quicker than I expected. This isn't a reflection on his performance. And I don't want to go into all the sordid details, although I'm sure many would like to know. Being on tour can be exhausting, so I didn't fault him for wanting to call it a night. I needed to get home too; my parents always waited up for me.

Most girls often visualize their first time and fantasize what it might be like. My first time was much different than I expected. He didn't say "I love you" or "Thanks for sharing that with me." He did say, "Now, don't do this with anyone else."

I told him that I wanted to see him again, and he said he wanted to as well. Then I got dressed, left, and made it home by midnight. He wanted to walk me to my car, but I suddenly became embarrassed about that old Chevy I once drove proudly all over Liberty Township. On the drive home, I can't say I was on cloud nine or anything like that. Being with him that night just felt right. It was destiny. It was karma. I was where I was supposed to be and knew this was more than a one-night stand. This thing we had was sure to last for years to come.

When I got home, I tiptoed straight to bed. "Did you have a good time? Did you get to see Frankie at all?" my mom inquired from her room. "Yeah, Mom, thanks for letting me go. Night. Love you." I had school the next day. Nothing changed on the outside. I didn't have the after-sex glow. On the inside, though, everything was somehow profoundly different.

Sleeping with him sealed the deal. Like I said, I really loved him. I used to tell Frankie all the time how much I loved him. I didn't act shy about it either. I would look him straight in the eyes (I knew the importance of eye contact and a clear voice), and I just said it. I'm not sure that he believed me, or he didn't care. I still believe we should tell the people most dear to our hearts that we love them. What they do with that is not for us to decide, but put it out there, make the moments count; they fly by so quickly.

Frankie was interested in me. He called me. I called his agent. We hooked up several times a year. I loved him. After writing this, I'm beginning to wonder if I don't still love him.

The guys in the group were as polite as possible, given the set of circumstances. Bob Gaudio was gorgeous, educated, and very elegant. A little class and education goes a long way. Speaking of long, Joey Long was so kind in a quiet and gentle way. Then there was Mr. Tommy DeVito. He was represented very well on stage and screen. He was distantly polite and totally disinterested.

On one particular trip, I asked my mother to take me to Akron, about an hour from Youngstown, to meet up with Frankie's tour bus. I'll never forget what my mother said to him that day: "Take care of my daughter." He respectfully shook her hand.

Some may think it was ridiculous or neglectful for her to let me go. But I believe she thought he would take care of me. And I did too. My mother may have believed that he could truly love me, because in her eyes, she only saw the best in me. That meant a lot to me. I really honestly felt deep in my soul that he loved me. Why else would he want to see me again? In my young mind, it never occurred to me that I was his Ohio groupie, his hookup, his lay on the road. It never crossed my simple, naive mind that he only wanted me for a few days to be his love toy. That may sound a little stupid, but I wasn't stupid; I was trusting. Looking back, I wonder if my mom really wanted to get on that bus herself and ride away to a better life. Unfortunately, that's a conversation that will never take place.

I freaking don't know what I thought. I always got what I set my sights on. It was inconceivable to me that I wouldn't win his love. Naive or arrogant? I just thought he was a tough nut to crack, but nothing worth having comes easy. Although he did! LOL.

Seventeen-year-olds often have sex in a lot of places, and I was no different. While the average girl that age might sneak off to a basement, the park, or the back of a car, I made it every place a famous musician could. We made love in backstage dressing rooms, hotel rooms, tour buses, and limos. Think of a place that one of the most renowned musicians of all time might have sex, and we probably did the deed there. We even had sex on the tour bus, with people listening. That was a little embarrassing.

After the silent treatment and the way he left the room to talk, I caught on that he was meeting someone. Then, of course, Mary Ann was on the cover of his album. That really killed me. I went blond from that moment on. Then he goes and marries a brunette. As though my hair color would have made a difference to him.

After a few weeks, Frankie sent me home. I later caught on that another woman was meeting him. This happened again the following year. Yes, it bothered me, but I figured this was just something I had to endure while I waited for him. Two years later, when I was nineteen, he planned to take me to Hawaii. He and Mary Ann had divorced. I thought this might be my time, that he would make me the next Mrs. Frankie Valli.

I cheated by never allowing myself to give all my heart away. Does that make me incapable of committing? Or does it make me truly imprinted on this stupid little guy? Or is it love? What is love but a connection, a willingness to get carpet burn, and to puff up your eyes through boundless tears. Did I cheat myself? Did I cheat everyone who tried to get close to me? Perhaps true imprints cause us to be trouble for love. He was the song in my heart, the color in my cosmetic bag of tricks. I couldn't think of regrets. I had to stay focused as a type A chick with my head held up high, staying with what I knew. Perhaps the rest was a facade of darkness, a part I played on my stage, saying goodbye in words but never in my soul.

But before we left, Frankie's daughter died. We never went to Hawaii. The fates seemed to have intervened, once again blocking this relationship. I've wondered a few times over the years how things would have been different. I'm sure I could have made him happy. He was everything to me. Everything.

I did anything—not just sexually—that he wanted, because deep in my heart, I believed I would one day become the next Mrs. Frankie Valli. I slept with him on and off for the next twenty years because I loved him. But my love for him undermined my marriages as well as the choices of all the men I fell for. Remember, this was in the '70s in Bomb Town, USA, Youngstown, Ohio, where Mafia figures were idolized rather than rejected. The attraction to Italian men with gold and a swagger made many women, me included, weak and wet. The beautiful girls married these men, joined the country club, had babies, and turned their heads from what their husbands did. The characters hanging around posh restaurants and dance clubs were very similar to those complex bad guys we all love from *The Godfather*, *The Sopranos*, or *Boardwalk Empire*. Suitors who were clean-cut, honest, sincere, and just plain nice didn't interest me. Some were intelligent, stand-up guys who really cared for me and would have given me a wonderful life. As I look back, I regret nonchalantly passing on some of the super men who wanted a committed relationship with me. I rejected them all because I kept looking for a substitute for Frankie.

I once heard Shirley MacLaine say that we fall down in love from the crown chakra, meaning that the mind creates first and the rest of the body reacts. I was physically quite shaken, and probably still am on some level, when I realized Frankie was a man with many lovers and little loyalty. I waited decades for him to realize how much I loved him. I felt I would love him into this, come hell or high water. There's a joke that's pretty accurate about men versus women. It goes like this: a man marries a woman and hopes she never changes; a woman marries a man and can't wait to change him.

But time passed. I moved on—I needed to if I wanted to have any chance at the kind of long-lasting, happily-ever-after relationship that every girl dreams of.

When I fell for Frankie, I lacked so much in my personal life. I needed someone to love me. In my immature mind, I deserved to be loved by him. He imprinted on me. I wasted my whole life imprinted, following a person who's not, in my estimation, a good fit for me. My relationship with Frankie—and I'm not here to bash him continually—affected my values, goals, and concept of what kind of man I envisioned would make me happy. Yes, I loved him, but I realize now that loving him has hindered me for nearly my entire life.

Many young women project a false vision of their Prince Charming and fall in love with the wrong guy. As a young girl, we have a vision of what our hero or knight in shining armor should look like. We want them to cherish us. Put us on a throne. Care for us. Love us. Protect us. After what I went through, I want to warn others about the powerful effect of romantic imprinting. I wish someone would have had something available forty years ago that might have helped me. Unfortunately, kids are subjected to sexual ideas so much younger due in part to social media, and I would wager a bet nine to one that this issue is not going away, but growing in the hearts of young men as well as women and will continue to have adverse effects on their love lives as adults.

I want to reach out to those who have also unconsciously cemented a false ideal of their beloved at an early age. They don't understand the immense power of these subconscious drives, plunging many into serial divorces, affairs, and living in delusion. The statistics of affairs are still high, with an increase in more women seeking intimacy outside the marital bedroom than ever before. This risk-taking behavior destroys the core of our self-esteem and, on a larger scale, society itself. Whether it's the Holiday Inn in Ohio or the Delano in South Beach, turning that key to find love or using sex as a distraction to unhealed issues can be deadly and self-destructive, especially when this desire is based on your inner child's ideal partner. Think about it: would you let a seven-year-old pick out your life partner? A child's values and cognitive thought processes aren't fully developed. And I'm not bashing celebrities; your imprint could be with an author, someone in politics, or a big brother's best friend. It doesn't matter. The point is that your inner child imprints and hangs around lingering in your adult subconscious encouraging you to believe their magical beliefs about love and sexuality. The fault is truly then only ours. We are often the creator of our own heartaches.

A woman's strength comes from her father. I have witnessed as a woman, a mother, a guidance counselor, and a social worker that there is black hole in the core of a woman when she doesn't have her dad when she is growing up. My uncle Larry would always send his daughter one rose each Valentine's Day. My dad never did that. A lot of dads don't. They come home exhausted, resentful, and who knows what, and they wonder why their little girls dress like whores, are boy crazy, and marry too young. Without a father, the words we need to hear aren't there, the shoes we need to step into are missing, the pieces of our hearts don't fit quite right. Where are the words from Dad that will get us through and make it OK? The role of a daddy is teaching his daughter that she is strong, courageous, and able to handle what life throws at her. He models a male image that is kind and respectful. Men, you have no idea what happens when you leave the responsibility of raising the kids to moms. Worse yet, I didn't have a grand-father or uncle or close family friend who loved me like a dad. Instead, I fell in love with a celebrity.

Every human being alive today—strong or weak, independent or codependent, wealthy or poor—wants to be loved, especially in the last century when romance and the idea of soul mates took center stage. Nothing has been quite the same since.

Of course, you will always find some who will avoid intimacy altogether, suppressing their needs or projecting them on careers or service. But for most of us silly romantics, we keep on trying no matter how many cracks our hearts get, and we tell ourselves that this is a "normal" part of the process. Neither is a healthy way to live.

I have since realized that I was a fool to wait for Frankie Valli. After my divorce, I went back to him. Like always, I pursued him. I admit that and take full responsibility as the adult I am today.

I kept hoping that he'd ask me to be his wife. Obviously, he never did. I never asked him to leave any of his wives. In doing everything that he asked, everything he told me—always stay beautiful, don't let yourself go, don't do drugs, go to college, don't talk too much—I was doing everything I needed to make him want me forever. But he didn't. Now I have to live with that.

I started to get over Frankie Valli and was most riveted to that dark place that I kept hidden for so long when I saw a picture of him with his new girlfriend. Oh my God, she's a baby. She's a child. He's eighty. What? My mind raced. She was young, much younger than him, simply dressed, short hair, and wearing unassuming jewelry. I paused and had to read the words under the photo two or three times. The plain Jane looked more like Frankie's son's friend. They say one picture is worth a thousand words. For me it was worth thousands of dollars in therapy. This press photo from a magazine was like a hit man putting a bullet between my eyes. I stopped dead in my tracks and realized, my Lord, it wasn't that I was too young for him; it was that he never liked me. I was never going to be good enough for him, let alone be his wife or even be respected by him or anyone who knew about us. I was, in my mind, reduced to being nothing but an Ohio groupie or worse. What I found out later about Frankie's behavior still wreaks havoc in my mind. I haven't quite recovered from it still. I'm hurt, disappointed, and dismayed. Like a healed gunshot wound, it seems to others I'm unaffected, but the scar tissue is still underneath, pulsating and reminding me to wise up and move on.

I pinned my hopes and dreams on a man who would never love me even if I had moved to Hollywood or New York and become a successful actress. I should win an Oscar for the role I played as a delusional overemotional woman looking for love in all the wrong places. How many of us are actors going through our days, playing roles as if on autopilot? We create in our heads what we think is best, ignoring signs of disaster up ahead. We are often the most destructive to our highest personal growth. And I'm not alone in that regard. Many women wait—and hope—for that one special guy to give themselves to while others give it away to everyone, each trying in their own way to find their way back to love. But they often don't find him. Then they settle for second best, pressured by birthdays and the fear of growing old alone. Day after day, year after year, the woman is left with a heart that has a pin-sized leak staining the lives of all who see the spots and cautiously move around them. No one is immune, and no one but the woman herself can remove the splatters of her sorrow.

These romantic mistakes and misfortunes in our lives not only alter us, but our family and our children's futures as well. This is imprinting.

Well, it turns out that my knight in shining armor, my Prince Charming, was not Frankie Valli. I've often wondered, not as much as I did when I was younger, what would have happened if we had gone to Hawaii. It was the first time Frankie suggested a trip that didn't revolve around a concert tour. Tragically, his daughter passed, and all connections with him slipped away. The darkness and despair that anyone experiences when they lose a child makes everyone and everything else fade into the shadows. If the fates had not closed this door, with Frankie's permission, I might be writing this book about the glamorous life of being Mrs. Frankie Valli. Who knows? Oh, the road not taken always seems more enchanting!

So having not won Frankie, I did what most young women do at that age, I looked for someone similar. We've all done that, right? We've settled for the second, third, or maybe even fourth version of the first guy who swept us off our feet. Let's face it, most of us go to class reunions to catch a glimpse of the one who first stole our heart.

Instead of being with Frankie, I returned to a normal Midwest high school life, attending football games, going out on Friday nights with girlfriends, looking for guys. One night after a game, my cousin Kathy, nine months younger than me, and I managed to sneak into a swanky Italian restaurant called Alberini's. It had an attached bar, so it was easy to get in without being carded. There was a live band playing, and the place was packed. We always pushed the envelope together, and if we got in a jam, we could always call on Aunt Ginny to rescue us. Some things never change. It was a time in America when you could play pranks like toilet paper houses without going to jail. We always left the keys in the ignition of our cars and seldom felt scared of anything but our ability to get ourselves out of trouble without telling our parents. Kathy was so opposite of me and wouldn't take anyone at face value or put up with their bullshit. In fact, if she got mad at a boyfriend, she'd put him into her trunk to teach him a thing or two. What a pistol!

The first substitute who swept me off my feet was a gentleman by the name of Marc Lawrence Fandano. Remember, I was all about the Italians at that time. In some ways, I still am.

There is something about European men that draws me to them. Italian men are in love with love, just like me I suppose. After all, I'm half Italian. Romance is in their DNA, and a lovely woman on their arm is invigorating to them. They are inspired by music, great food, their mamas, and a slow dance. They dress impeccably and see an expensive home and high-end cars like a Lincoln Continental or a Corvette as sound investments, not so much their women.

Kathy and I strode into Alberini's dressed all grown-up in our polyester suits and heels. My Farrah Fawcett haircut danced softly on my shoulders when I walked past a line of grown-up boys. My Frankie Valli gold album necklace hung around my neck while my hippie-chick pale-rose-colored glasses sat at the tip of my nose. We worked our way to the bar, and I ordered a Pepsi. I was nervous about getting carded and would have died of embarrassment had we been asked to leave. We weren't at the bar very long when this Tom Selleck look-alike sauntered over and said, "Hi, beautiful. Take off your glasses so I can see your eyes."

While Kathy laughed, I fell into a trance. Marc edged into my space and whispered, "I just want you to know something. I'm going to marry you. Remember this moment." Maybe that was why Kathy took her rattail comb and stuck holes in the tires of Marc's big gold Cadillac a year later when we were having a lover's spat.

There on the dance floor, we moved in unison to the Bee Gees' disco beat. At that moment, I thought that maybe, just maybe, someone other than Frankie could make the magic happen. And maybe this guy would love me back.

I met Marc in between Frankie and graduating from high school. I had already been accepted to Oral Roberts University in Tulsa, Oklahoma for the fall of 1976. Unfortunately, I was totally unprepared for what I was getting myself into. I couldn't stand the murals of Oral Roberts. Where are the murals of Christ? I pondered as I walked across that majestic campus. Isn't this supposed to be about spirituality? My mind began to shut down the possibility that this could ever be considered my home for the next four years. And the rules! Good gracious. Boys could do everything, and the ladies had curfews and dress codes. I know hate is a strong word, but I am a rule-follower because I want to be, not because someone demands it of me. There's a bit of a rebel in me.

But the cold hard truth was I that didn't give Oral Roberts University a chance, and I was scared to be out of my fishbowl. That's why it's best to make kids stick it out the first year away from home. Fear will cause even those most capable of success to run for safety and hide. With the crap going on at home and the constant fighting between my mom and my stepdad, I couldn't handle the challenges of striking with a strong emotional foundation. I found myself with my high school diploma in one hand and my suitcase in the other, emotionally unprepared, lacking so many social skills required to do what I needed to do. According to the purple cow and my mom, I was groomed to be a star, but I didn't know how to leave home or where I was supposed to go. I realize that probably doesn't make sense, because goal-oriented individuals are supposed to be excited to leave home and conquer the world, but nothing could have been farther from the truth. It's unrealistic to believe stars are discovered in their own backyards or while attending prayer meetings in a town of ten thousand people. But that was the dichotomy of my life. I missed the tryouts I earned for the Dallas cheerleaders. I canceled my audition at Fordham University in NYC. I shorted myself. I was afraid.

I was told over and over and over and over one more time, "Be ready. Walk straight. Don't swing your arms, crack gum, or dress like trash. You're not trash. You are wonderful. Make us proud."

I now understand that having to try to be both kinds of

people is impossible, though I gave it my best. I tried to make my mom proud. I really did. The pain in her eyes from her demons consumed her, and I was left without a parent to guide me. Still, I made up my mind at a young age that I wouldn't disappoint. The rules under which I was raised to be a famous saint were the code embedded into my core. I find a strange peace in calling it out and giving it a name as who I truly am—a sexy saint. Is that even possible? Yes, it is. I'm living proof. This tale is not one about self-pity, but more of the courage to come out with my authentic self and share what I have learned. I was emotionally unprepared to parent the Queen Bee. When there are no real grown-ups in the room, you do the best you can.

Like many families born of codependence, my mom eagerly brought me back home, and my aunt was there waiting to go out dancing. I quickly transferred to Bowling Green State University in Bowling Green, Ohio. The 175 miles that separated us was much more manageable for my entire family and Marc. Much to my disappointment, I soon discovered that I didn't fit in at Bowling Green either. I didn't know how to act. I didn't drink or sleep with guys, so I was out of the loop. You can say that I was a late bloomer in many ways, yet an old soul in other areas. Another dichotomy in my life.

Marc, twelve years my senior, seduced me and presented a view of himself that wasn't always correct. I think he wanted to be that person; I know I wanted him to be as well. He said his last name was Fandano and that he practiced law in Cleveland. He actually even gave me a golden gavel to wear around my neck. Of course I believed him until my stepdad took his license plate number and found that he was a local guy with a regular forty-hour-a-week job and a wife who belonged to a local prominent family in the political and legal world. For the record, that woman and I have become somewhat kindred souls, traveling down a road crossing at many junctures. She is the very same woman that was my future boyfriend's first crush in Catholic school. Synchronicity is everywhere if you are awake and watch for the signs.

Frankie never did that to me. He was the opposite, and that may have been one of the reasons that I felt we were supposed to be together. Frankie openly told me about his relationships as though he wanted to come clean somehow. He vented about what he said to Mary Ann when she wrecked his car. I could sense that Frankie was still fuming as he recounted how he instructed the maid to get Mrs. Valli on the phone when she refused to pick up the line. On another trip, years later, Frankie discussed his thoughts about Randy and his intentions to ask for her hand in marriage. He always seemed eager to share details about his love after we made love. I couldn't wrap my head around why he would say these very personal things to me. He did it again after he divorced Randy. "I will never get married again, and I'm leaving all my money to my kids." Gee, thanks for sharing. Not!

Breathless and stunned, I always sat on the side of the bed, wrapped in the sheets, knowing that once again I was considered only Ms. Almost Good Enough. This had become a recurring nightmare upon returning home after brief stays with this legend. As always, he strutted around naked and then showered. I grew silent and withered as quickly as a flower in the heat. Hearing the shower water shut off, I always wiped my tears and regained my composure before he came out of the bathroom. I chanted this mantra long before I ever read Deepak Chopra, "If I'm good enough, he will let me stay," over and over, giving me strength to persevere. Perhaps he will ask me to be by his side as his friend, his lover, his confidante, part of his family. We will set the world on fire and demonstrate what love songs are about, I convinced myself.

Marc is one man who kept his word: "I'm going to marry you." We got married in early June 1978. That year, Kiss was the most popular band on the planet, Bob Crane died, *The Six Million Dollar Man* and *The Bionic Woman* were canceled, the Blues Brothers made their debut on *Saturday Night Live*, and *Grease* topped the box office. My aunt Larene, my mom's sister, tried to convince me that I was too young to get married. I would have none of it. Nineteen at the time, I thought Marc was what I needed in a man. Notice I didn't say wanted.

My mother was heartbroken that I wouldn't listen to my aunt Larene, so she passed the baton of wedding-planning duties to my aunt Ginny. A college freshman, I was too young to plan a wedding that should never have taken place.

But I wanted Marc. He impacted my personality in ways that I didn't discover or understand until years later. Growing up, my family wasn't wealthy, but whatever money they had, I got. My grandma saved green stamps for Christmas gifts starting in July. We never belonged to any social clubs. We only attended church functions. My grandma was saved by the time I was born, so the life I knew was wholesome, tender, and kind, nestled down that gravel road in that small farmhouse in the woods. We never had fish, but we had a lot of chicken. Fried chicken, chicken and dumplings, chicken and noodles, chicken pot pies. The fact that I live in Florida and don't eat fish blows people away, but I just never acquired a taste for it. Crazy how early childhood still navigates our choices even as grown-ups residing in a totally new environment. We always had a garden, and I must say that I'm quite competent at snapping green beans. My favorite sandwich comes toasted and lightly buttered, with salt and pepper and tomato slices without any meat inside—the poor man's sandwich. I laugh now with a fond remembrance of days gone by. I've grown to embrace my childhood, even the simplest of traditions.

I wore the most expensive clothes growing up, but my mom and her sisters wore hand-me-downs. Our family saved for one good car and one work car. My parents didn't believe in racking up debt. We paid cash for everything, a lesson that many today should learn, in my opinion. By this time, my mom worked at Packard Electric due to her divorce. She had to make a living, and this job had the highest wages in the Trumbull County area. The line work caused her hands to bleed, and she had to get up at 4:00 a.m. every day for years and years. It was awful to watch her almost collapse from exhaustion each night. The factories were dark, smelly, and rough. The opposite of my mom, who was fair, fragile, and delicate. The job provided excellent health insurance and a safe retirement plan for someone without a college education. Many felt she hit the jackpot. I think this was the first step to her demise. She wanted to wear beautiful dresses to work and live with a bit of class. Nonetheless, she loved her kids more than herself, so she stuck it out. One thing I have to say: the women in our family have a history of being hard workers, strong willed and determined to do whatever it took for their kids. My aunt Ginny worked in the offices at Packard Electric as well.

Most of Grandma's kids had moved out of the house, so I spent a lot of time there while my mom worked. Eventually, my cousin Heather, Aunt Ginny's daughter, was there a lot when her mom worked at Delphi too. Years of walking to school together up that gravel hill throughout all the seasons still resonate within my being. I love the seasons and often find myself leaving Florida and wandering home to Ohio in search of the smells of freshly cut grass and crispy fall leaves burning and the cool air going in my nose after the first snow. Like the first remembrances that hold a unique place in my being, I was the first granddaughter, and like all "firsts," I had a special space in Grandma's heart. I remember the years we drove together to Ravenna for baton lessons with this champion twirler. The last day before I finally quit, she was profoundly moved by emotion. Funny, at the time I never knew it. Years later, when my mom passed, I found a letter she wrote to me. It was scribbled on faded paper in the back of my Frankie Valli scrapbook, misspelled and filled with unconditional love.

July 25, 1972

Today I lost my little girl, we had our last baton lesson in Ravenna.

I feel very depressed at the same time I feel so very, very, very, blest to have had her these past 14 1/2 years.

I can only do one thing now, that is to leave her in the hands of God and pray he will cover her with the blood of Jesus and put a wall of fire around her.

It will be hard to remember me, I'm only her old fashioned Grandma that is kind of square.

All my love to you Princess.

Please God take care of her and I'll be grateful throughout all of eternity.

Just Gram

As a late bloomer, I stayed close to Gram and Mom and Gigi. When I finally quit those baton lessons in Ravenna, Ohio, my grandma must have thought of it as a rite of passage of sorts. In truth, we didn't go out together much more after that. Soon, I got my driving permit and was driving all over with the radio blaring like a silly teenager. Saying goodbye to your kids is so tough. You want them to be grown, but you don't. The day Dana got married, I imagined all the similar scenarios I put my family through. They seemed to have survived, I thought. I must too! When my mom was dying, I cried and asked why.

She said, "This is life, April Lynn." She always called me April Lynn. No one does that anymore. Funny, the weird things you miss.

CHAPTER 4

Who Loves You, Pretty Baby

Marc introduced me to a lifestyle that I didn't know existed. He came from wealth. His parents lived in Dade County, Florida, which was known for lush living and golf courses like Doral Country Club. Marc's aunt was Annette Chesebrough of Chesebrough Manufacturing Company, which merged in 1955 with Pond's cold cream, Cutex, and Matchabelli perfumes. Marc's uncle was one of the key players in the creation of the year-round jai alai operations, including Miami Jai-Alai Fronton (the biggest in the world, with a record audience of 15,502 people on December 27, 1975).

Marc loved to golf, and as an only child, he usually got what he wanted, which included me. He loved everything about me the minute he met me. The way I looked. The way I talked. The way I walked. Today, I see how much I actually resemble his mother. She was spunky, incredibly classy, and also spoiled beyond belief. I'm not sure if he created in me some of her or if I am indeed very much like Rose. A grand dame she was, and I feel in great company being compared to her.

Listen to how this guy not only made me weak in the knees, but made me fall on the floor. The first night we met, I mentioned that I didn't own many albums. Digital music was years away from being the preferred means of listening to music, and cassettes were just on the verge of taking over the market. I only owned a few Four Seasons records. The day after I shared this with Marc, he had forty-eight albums delivered to my house. I don't remember the names of all of them, but I do remember Boz Scaggs; Three Dog Night; Chicago; Bread; the Temptations; Earth, Wind & Fire; and, the most romantic, Barry White.

In another innocent conversation, I mentioned that I was scheduled for an interview the following day. The next morning, a new suit from a pricey boutique was delivered to my doorstep. And it went on and on until I was charmed by his larger-than-life, grandiose gestures. I mean, this guy didn't miss a beat. He knew how to wine and dine a woman, and that woman was me. Honestly, he had me at hello.

Living away from home wasn't comfortable for me. I felt out of my element. I was pretty enough. But I was lost. I couldn't talk to people right. I wanted my aunt Ginny. I wanted to be safe. Besides, Bowling Green State University is out in the sticks, with flat land that made the winters unbearable. I hate the cold. And the acting classes just proved to me I wasn't an actor. I wasn't anything. I didn't know who I was. I thought about going into radio or TV, but I cut my finger in a tape machine, and it scared me. I loved that field, and that was what I should have done as a career. It is something I'm great at. I had a job at a radio station and took the book from a 3.1 to a 9.0 my first time out. Another mistake. I still think that being an entertainer would have been a super fit for me. Another time, another place, should have, could have, but didn't follow through. I didn't fight for it.

I also lived in freshman Founders Hall with two farm girls.

We argued about how to dust and vacuum. Do we vacuum first? Do we dust first? It was terrible. I gained eight pounds. Now I hate being fat. That was the topper. If I look fat, I want to die. I admit it.

I heard Frankie was anorexic and had this thing of eating only maple syrup. Now that's only a rumor. But for those of us who have been praised for our tiny frames, I get it. I heard he went into heart failure due to that. The pressure of having to be successful is stressful. If my toenail breaks, I go running to the salon. How much running can we do before we collapse? Perfection is an impossible goal. Perfection is a delusion. I myself like staying alone more and enjoying the ducks, the squirrels, and the bunny I feed every morning. Silence is golden; Frankie taught me that!

Perfection is fickle by definition, which makes it changeable and worthless. Short hair, cut if off. Long hair, get extensions. Big boobs, we can fix that. Big booty, got that covered too. One thing we don't have covered is stupid; another is shallow. We still strive for it nonetheless. That's a problem with being a beautiful woman; many doors open and not all of them benefit her highest personal growth and empowerment.

When I met Marc, I still think I loved Frankie, but like any teenager, being treated like royalty by such a handsome older man put me into the here and now. How many eighteen-year-old girls get flown to Chicago for dinner at the Playboy Club? Looking back and seeing so much of myself in Marc, I now see that I was Marc's imprint. For Marc, I was his one and only. I regret that I didn't understand what was going on back then. In retrospect, it feels to me that I was dishonest to him. I could have chosen to date him and enjoy him, but not to vow my love to him. You can't give something away you no longer have. I could have walked the walk about integrity instead of the bullshit we feed ourselves and everyone in listening distance. I used him to get away from Bowling Green, and from my mom and my stepdad, Les. I blamed them for me marrying Marc, but I made myself a prisoner to lies.

I am a woman who honors truth more than any virtue, and this cuts deeply in my memory, tainting so many of the wonderful moments we shared. I so honor his deep sentiment for me and will always look at him with deep fondness.

I was never in love with Marc, but I really loved him, if that makes sense. He looked like the perfect groom on top of a wedding cake. My very own Tom Selleck. Yes, that sounds cheap, but eighteen-year-olds are shallow if nothing else. We all have a vision in our heads of what our ideal mate would be like and that includes appearance. Let's face it, for love to blossom, there has to be some sexual tension, that erotic dance of passion between lovers that makes it impossible to stop touching and fondling one another. It's a type of temporary insanity that drives us to make stupid decisions and lacks all cognitive common sense. Marc was and still is a gorgeous man, even after he got out of prison. I think we made the best-looking couple of all my lovers. It did irritate me though when he needed more room in our closet for his clothes than mine. That's just not cool! I also don't ever want to sleep with a man whose hair is longer than mine. No, no, no!

Even so, Marc introduced me to a better lifestyle, and I admit that way of life is still important to me. It was a romantic time in my life. He took me to five-star restaurants night after night. At every restaurant we went to, he had the orchestra play the Italian wedding song. It was charming. He always surprised me with just-because gifts that I didn't expect, which, to every woman, is the best kind of surprise. It was pretty tempting to be loved like that. Marc bought me my first Louis Vuitton and introduced me to South Florida, visiting Worth Avenue and Bal Harbor.

I was his imprint. His vision of his perfect mate. Isn't it nice to know, ladies, that this imprinting business has no gender bias? We were at lunch a few years ago and he said, "Out of all the women in my life, you to me were the perfect match, my ideal vision of a woman. I only blame your mother that we didn't make it work, not you." Many times we don't become aware of the effect of imprinting until years later. When this happened to me, pop psychology wasn't trendy. Back then, even the idea of going to a therapist was synonymous to being thrown in a padded cell, getting shock treatments, and living the rest of your life in an overmedicated fog. Well, the overmedicated thing is still alive and thriving, but today, seeking wellbeing is almost like receiving a badge of honor for striving to be your very best self. Today, everyone in the know has at least one concierge service at their beck and call. Today it's all about the mind, soul, body connection. Hopefully everyone is sincere.

Looking back, I can say that no one has ever loved me as much as Marc. He loved me unconditionally, even when I tried to break up with him. Each time I tried to gently pull away, he would do something to lure me back. One night when we just stated seeing another, he came over to my aunt and uncle's, knocking on the door very late, singing Lou Rawls's "You'll Never Find Another Love Like Mine." My aunt and uncle gushed, and so did I the next morning when they told me about his craziness. My uncle Chuck made up this word, Gattafied. My maiden name is Gatta. The word means bewitched by me, done in, fallen and lost in a sea of romance. With a man so entranced, I myself couldn't resist his calls to his arms. So each time, I went back to him.

We got married in June, a spring day with country wild-flowers, in a tiny Christian church with all Marc's family from Miami in attendance. Our rehearsal dinner was at the restaurant where we first met, Alberini's. I wore a gown that was very much like my mom's. White lace, fitted bosom, full skirt, with a stunning long train. I wanted that! Despite all the craziness with my mother, I wanted to be a beautiful bride like her. With all the mixed messages, the fights, the heartache, I knew this woman couldn't wrap her head around her issues but lived for me and loved me in spite of herself.

The day of my wedding to Marc, a very influential bookie called the house about an hour before I was to walk down the aisle. I'm slipping into my wedding dress, my bridesmaids are dressed and helping me, and this guy calls! He told my step-father that he knew me, that I was a beautiful girl, and that my husband-to-be was one of the worst and biggest gamblers that he has ever known. Of course, this is information that would have been more beneficial more than an hour before we took our vows. I dismissed it and pretended the call never came through and looked hopeful on the drive as the limousine took me to my future husband. I walked down the aisle to marry Marc in front of three hundred guests. Anyone who was anyone attended. Italian weddings are better attended than most family reunions. A person can skip a family reunion. No one skips an Italian wedding or a wake.

During the ceremony, our unity candle blew out. Maybe God was trying to show me that our marriage was over before it started. Like all brides though, I thought my marriage was the beginning of something wonderful. And it could have been if I wasn't too young, as we were a rather perfect match. Marc was twelve years my senior, so he fit in perfectly with Aunt Ginny and Uncle Chuck. Even the silly teenage pranks I did made them laugh. One time I was so mad at Marc that I dumped a pitcher of beer on his head. He then poured one on me. I was shocked, and I loved his passion to do it back.

The Gatta/Pagano reception took place at the top of the mall in a very swanky Italian restaurant. The wine-colored curtains, striped upholstery, oversized chandeliers everywhere, and candles on linen-covered round tables kept it dim and romantic. It was a huge party that only true Italians can pull off. Polka, tarentelle, the wedding dance pinning dollars on my gown. It was loud, of course, as all Italians parties are. Food was overflowing, and there were cookie tables everywhere and top-shelf liquor. The celebration filled the room with dancing and laughter, all except my mother, who was solemn. The train on my dress was so long it got ripped during the reception. I could barely walk by the end, but Aunt Ginny and Uncle Chuck made sure we didn't stop until way into the morning. Think the wedding scene from *The Godfather*. My dad paid for most of it, and he was proud I married an Italian after all the grief my grandma put him and his family through. I never really thanked him for that, probably because I am still disappointed in myself for marrying so young and wasting his money.

Our marriage didn't even last long enough for the ink to dry on the marriage license. We lived in a little apartment at the end of the street where I grew up. Not good, I know. Too close to dear old Mom. Remember words like codependent and boundaries weren't common terms back then. I was still going to college, so I really didn't cook. I was too young to get married. I remember crying three days before the wedding. I knew I shouldn't marry Marc, but as was the case many times in my life, I didn't have anywhere else to go.

I hated feeling trapped. Have you ever felt so trapped that you just kept making things worse for yourself? That's what happened to me. This was the first of many times I would tell myself, "I don't want to go, but I can't stay." I ran from my mom's issues to a person who had another sort of addiction. All addictions are destructive to everyone involved. No one is spared. Addiction is a sort of poison seeping onto the floor, touching everyone in the home, taking no prisoners. All I ever wanted is to feel safe, and here I was involved with a major-league gambler. Either we were living like kings with thousands in cash, or we were broke, eating out through the help of Visa without a penny to our names. I was attending Youngstown State University full-time, so I didn't work. After a few bouts of feast or famine, I got nervous and began to wake up and smell the rotten garbage stinking up my home. I was in a mess. I tried, like all young brides, to keep on keeping on, but shit still stinks no matter what bag you put it in. With all the short-term fixes I explored, the problem always reared its ugly head in the morning.

Besides, I was a mere child and not ready for a lifelong commitment to anything and not willing to sacrifice all it would have taken to confront Marc about his issues. At that point I wasn't even sure of my issues, let alone his. In addition, I had no real role models of what a happy wife was like.

Beverly Jean was a debutante of sorts in her own mind and those of her many admirers. Her dream was never to be a housewife working at Delphi Packard Electric. I think it would have suited her better to be an airline stewardess or a secretary for some impressive law firm. So she struggled in a dark factory, hotter than hell in the summer and freezing in the winter. The hours were long, the piecework on the conveyors wrapping auto wires cut her hands, and her hair smelled of rubber. She struggled hoping to have someone or someplace offer refuge from her fears and personal anguish. The Queen Bee looked for peace with the men who loved her, the children she loved, and the church where she cried waiting for salvation. Unfortunately, she was too smart for that old-time religious dogma and looked boldly in the eyes of preachers and their threats of hell and damnation sermons. Their quotes and sermons only left her hollow inside.

The chaos in her mind spilled over into her relationship with my stepfather. If they argued once a week, it was a blissful environment. The arguments escalated into fist-fights, car chases, furniture flying, and police calls. It got to be kind of funny as adults when we saw his clothes going back and forth into the trunk. They knew just where to go. The courthouse was also a frequent friend of our family. My parents filed and canceled their divorce every six months for years. That's got to be in the Guinness Book of Get Me Out of Here. They were miserable together, and eventually no one wanted to come to our house. The tension was like a cloud that had descended upon our home, poisoning the air we breathed. Anyone who came close started to choke with dysfunction and inner confusion. No one used the built-in pool. One day my mom got so mad while my stepdad was at work that she had people come and fill it in with dirt. That's how insane it all was. My mom would send herself to the hospital for rest and to recoup from the latest explosion. The long-term effects are multigenerational, and still the rings of smoke whirl around us now and then.

I didn't even open a joint checking account with Marc. He golfed. I went to class. He got quiet. I got anxious. We had a tiny, furry shih tzu roommate, Lovebug, my little girl dog with big brown eyes, blond hair, bows, and clothes, and we both adored her. Aunt Ginny and Uncle Chuck got married in Vegas right after, and we both stood up for them, continuing our nonstop '70s party. We always hung out with them, and that made me feel safe and comfortable. I couldn't have gotten through most of my life without them. They are dotted here and there throughout all the events of my life . . . and that includes my relationships with men. Aunt Ginny and Uncle Chuck are all about living and making each day count for the best. I needed that then. I need it now.

I was developmentally lost in how to maximize the most of each day joyfully and fully. My mom was never like that. She hated my stepfather. She hated her job. She hated herself most of all. She always wanted to be somewhere else, anywhere else, and I'm still not sure why. It still makes me weepy to think she lived such an awful life, and I'm afraid I will follow in her worn-out, miserable pattern. It is a lifelong challenge, ridding ourselves of the patterns of early childhood.

The marriage of Mr. and Mrs. Marc Pagano didn't survive it for three reasons; it's never just one reason, though we like to believe it is. I suspect some of these are universal reasons love withers and divorce lawyers remain in high demand. Perhaps you will see parts of yourself or someone you know in the gloomy end. For one, I was just nineteen, far too young to truly understand how to make a marriage work. Unfortunately, now that I look back from a wiser perspective, Marc probably loved me the most. To this day, I would bet, one hundred to one, that he would leave anything and everything to be with me.

I don't think I was committed enough to him at nineteen. Looking back now, I never really had both feet in the relationship. I was just too young, and I got married for all the wrong reasons. I needed to get out of my family's house. I hated dorm life at Bowling Green. I had to escape the fighting with my mom and Les. Each week seemed more like a scene from Nightmare on Townsend Avenue. Teeth being knocked out, numerous police calls, hitting, threats of taking the money, ridiculous rules about window blinds, car mileage, et cetera, et cetera. It was toxic. I knew that much. My aunt Ginny helped by taking me on brief vacations to get away from it all.

Les started off being abusive, and my mom quickly picked up where he left off. I once heard they went to jail because Mom took a hatchet and smashed his car. It was my daughter's birthday. My aunt couldn't believe it and went to see for herself. There they were, sitting like two giant pumpkins, all orange.

The only hospitable family function we ever had was the burial of my mom. My stepfather has been a saint since then, helping me with my son. It makes you wonder if some people just are too toxic for one another and if divorce is better than hell on the home front. I lived in hell. I have since apologized to Les for the problems of our family life we all had a part of. It takes more than one person to let the elephant stay in the living room. Yes, it was awful. More than awful. How many times did I run across the street with my baby brother to get the police? By the way, my brother and I no longer speak, because he is appalled that I have written about our lives. Heart-rendingly sad for me. But now my stepfather has truly become the man every girl would want for a stepdad. He is simple, spending his time attending the church up the street and keeping my mom's house is running order. I hear him pray, asking for forgiveness, and cry when he speaks of the years when I was young and some of his most violent actions. Others judge me because I have moved on from the past. Isn't that we're supposed do? Church people have weird ideas.

Years later, I met Marc for lunch. He showed up with a bouquet of roses and had made reservations for a room in the hotel where we agreed to eat. During lunch, I shockingly realized that I still had this strange kind of mystical power over him. I decided to walk away because of how very much I genuinely cared for the man. In my hands was the power to control and manipulate. He was married at the time and had five children. I told him that I cared too deeply for him to let him destroy his life over his love for me. He respected my choice.

Another reason our marriage didn't make it was his little gambling problem. I did not realize what a gambler he was back then, or even that it was considered a full-blown destructive addiction. I'm not sure that I would have stuck with him, but I did call in my chips, calling it quits after a particularly unpleasant experience at an upscale restaurant called Somebody's in Austintown, Ohio. I grew accustomed to dining surrounded by fine linens, candlelight, champagne, and Italian music.

During the meal, Marc was greeted by two beefcake thugs with gaudy gold chains and big watches around their fat wrists. Their voices were more like pit bull growls, directly saying, "Please follow us to the back room where we can chat." I sensed the seriousness as Marc's self-tanned face instantly turned a pale greenish yellow. I was terrified standing there, watching Marc get roughed up in front of my very own eyes. I told them who my uncle was. My uncle worked for the railroad in downtown Youngstown where all the crooks and criminals hung out. I'm not sure if he was powerful, but he sure knew everyone. He was powerful in my eyes. Who can say what real power is? If he is powerful, perhaps it's because I give him power. From a chicken farm, everyone looks big and smart.

They permitted me to call him. Uncle Chuck asked to speak with the bookie then to Marc. In a few seconds, I was permitted to leave the room and wait at the table. I looked at Marc and walked quickly out of there, worried for both of us. I knew something really bad was going to happen if we didn't move fast. I feared for Marc's life. I didn't know this at the time, but I guess Marc had won $11,000 but had owed the bookie $5,000 for a very long time. A few minutes later, my uncle Chuck instructed Marc to leave the entire $11,000, keep his eyes down, and walk away. He came to pick me up at the table, and I quietly followed him out of the restaurant. He looked like he had been roughed up. His starched white shirt sported a drop of blood. The gold chain he wore that night was missing from his neck. It was a very long and quiet ride home. I sat silent.

When you live in a dysfunctional and emotionally abusive home, you kind of do crisis pretty well. It's day-to-day life that is new and unsettling to you. I was in shock. On the drive home, I knew it was time to end the mess that was our marriage. I left that night and went to my aunt Ginny's.

Years after my marriage to Marc ended, I had a natal life chart done by an astrologist. If I recall correctly, she stated the seventh house, the house of my first marriage, showed that it should have lasted but wouldn't, only because of karmic lessons and work yet to be done in the future. When we dated, Marc loved the idea of me, the thought of me, without even having to know me. Marc knew about my relationship with Frankie Valli, but he was so set on what he wanted that nothing would get in his way. I get that now. I was everything Marc always wanted. That's why I stay away from him.

I guess if you care for someone, really care, never give up hope always longing to see them they way you painted them in your mind. I was naive even the last time I saw Marc. I told him, "I'm so proud that you're a broker gambling with other people's money and have given up your obsession." Little did I realize, I'd hit the nail on the head. He was getting on a plane every week and going to Atlantic City to gamble. I believe he eventually got caught for US mail fraud. Addiction is everywhere. He is now divorced, with five kids, grandkids, and an elegant South Florida mother in Youngstown, Ohio, far from Dade Country, playing it big at the country club. I haven't seen him, but I bet he still looks so divine. Some people are genetically blessed with gifts. Stunningly handsome looks were his, brains not so much!

He called me again just last year after he got out of prison. His dad had since passed, and his mom came up to Ohio to save him from his financial ruin and public disgrace. I was shocked to hear his warm tones echoing like a melody after all these years. It's odd; the voice is so imitate to the heart, like an old song. He uttered warmly, "You know, you and I should have always been together." I laughed at his charm and accuracy. "Perhaps another lifetime." I held back wanting to share. I wasn't sure if he believed in reincarnation.

CHAPTER 5

Working My Way Back to You

Looking back, I see a lot of individuals, especially women, although men are by no means exempt, living in ways that are not true to their core essence. Family, religion, society, advertising, and partners tell us what to do, how to do it, and when to do it. The crazyass thing is that we let ourselves cave in to their demands, little by little, fading into the background, losing the authentic colors that once glowed and sparkled like diamonds out of our souls. I am barraged by others passing through my space with auras of pukey, pasty shades of beige, and I wonder what their story is, who stole their vibrancy, as I watch them uniformly pass by. But let's face it: no one can really enforce their "shoulds" and "musts" on someone else. Still, I have a sneaking suspicion that there's a lot of that going around. At least I am one of those who have let men sway my desires. Frankie Valli substitute number two was one who manipulated the bud off the tree before I even got to bloom. And substitute number three wanted to cut up my tree of life altogether if my goals were ever in conflict with his daily agenda.

I don't think I could have been coined a cougar back then, but Billy was only seventeen when we met at Youngstown State University, so I could have been one of the very first to don that crown. We performed in a play called Kismet together at Dana School of Music, Youngstown State University. The word kismet means fate.

Billy Kirkwood, my next substitute for Mr. Valli, was born December 20, 1960, in New Castle, Pennsylvania. He eventually became my second, and last, husband. Like me, he was from a poor working family. He wasn't Italian. He wasn't slick, though he definitely had a quiet coolness about him that was very sexy. He wasn't anything I thought I wanted, but I was thunderstruck when our eyes met. I believe we are from the same soul group and that this relationship was predestined. Oh God, we messed it up completely. I have written deeply in my soul's memory that I plan to make sure we have another go at it somewhere else in some other time. Billy stood six-foot-two, thin, great butt, and giant blue eyes, with wavy long hair. He was kind of full of it, but at first, I found his naive crap entertaining. In a tiny dive bar lined with pool tables near campus, we played Michael Jackson's "Rock with You" over and over and over until we were dizzy with passion and rum and Coca-Cola. We made love the first night we went out in his beat-up red car, wearing only my white cowboy boots. We saved those white silly boots for years like an Oscar symbolizing our love. It's the little things that make the big things guys do forgivable. His family hated me. Like all young lovers, hate is the ultimate motivator to run away and elope. You think parents would have learned that those tactics just don't work. Tell someone no, and watch them go butt-freaking nuts just to prove you wrong. I hate the word no.

If Billy's parents had only backed off and played it cool,

our relationship might have never deepened to any more than a college fling. You see, Miss Gypsy Rose, a.k.a. April Lynn, was getting more courageous. After my brief escapade with my handsome, broke-ass gambler, I finally felt like a woman ready to put my toe in the waters of the ocean of life. I was starting to really grow up, though I admit it was long overdue. Even away at college, with no one watching over me, I wouldn't let myself experiment and relax as a student. I still hold back to this day. Perhaps I'm scared to death of my dark side and what might just happen if I let her out to play. Have you ever danced with the devil in the pale moonlight? No, it's because if my dark side ever really comes out, I might lose control. But back then, a stirring had awakened in me, like rain pitter-pattering on the window, causing me to stir. I loved it. I had been baptized by fire, seeing firsthand the complex games men and women play, and found the rule book intoxicating and enticing. I wasn't ready to stay put in Ohio; there were greener pastures, and I had my go-go boots on. I wanted Cristal on South Beach wearing my Louboutin five-inch heels, with a slinky Herve Leger bandage dress. I was only twenty-one, and I was ready to sample what was on the other side. I loved dancing. Still do. I could go out dancing every night and never speak to a man. My love for dancing began when I was five. My mother dressed me up for weddings and family functions in frilly dresses so I wouldn't look too mature out on the dance floor. So I've had that spirit in me and it remains to this day, call it a curse or a gift!

I wanted to breathe and just be whatever I thought I wanted to be at that point in my life. Therapists say that whatever gaps we have missing developmentally we will go back and pick them up even though it's self-destructive on other levels. I agree. But I was also afraid. I loved Billy; I really did. As the love songs go, that kind of real connection doesn't happen along every day. I was young but not stupid. As I ponder on my past, I see that the worst moments in my life always happen when I am standing in the middle zone in the game of life. The gray area when I am nowhere but everywhere all at once. My mind swarms, wavering on blurting out yes or no, stay or go, move in or move out. After the decision is made, the rest seems to be almost anticlimactic, even when the world around me is in shock, while I dissemble parts of my life as others gaze in disbelief. My worst fear is that I am permanently in that middle zone, unable to reside anywhere else by my own choosing or lack thereof.

When Frankie called with an invite to Chicago, I was thrilled and filled with a drug called hope. The Bible tells us hope, faith, and charity are the crux of what living is for. I was ready to live then. Oh Lord, I felt like such a grown-up when I got my chance to once again dive into the life of Frankie as a real woman. I was cooler, wiser, much more fun, and able to speak an actual sentence with words that contained more than four syllables. I now find that being able to speak about diverse topics in groups is attractive, though I'm not sure he concurs or even cares what his ladies have to contribute to "manly" debates.

Frankie and I hadn't seen each other for four or five years, which seems like forever when you're young. He delightfully surprised me with the call. But when love comes calling, you jump, right? That's why I got furious with Mr. Billy when he interfered with my quest for the man of my dreams. Some events are bigger than the past, the present, and even the future, as though it has a life and cannot be ignored. In my mind, Frankie had waited for me to grow up. I wasn't his little plaything anymore. I was a real woman with real character, real style, real love to give him.

I wanted our reunion to be perfect. I went to Saks Fifth Avenue and bought beautiful casual-chic dresses with heels. Well, my mom did. I still had her credit cards, so I used them for my purchases. I returned home with bags on both arms, grinning like a cat who just swallowed the canary, or was about to.

During the plane ride, I convinced myself that Frankie had finally come to his senses and realized I was the one for him. I rarely traveled outside the state of Ohio with him. So I took this trip, somewhat of a replacement for the missed trip to Hawaii, as a sign we were going to the next level.

Why I thought that is beyond me. Once again, as I read the memories on these pages, I only know his voice made me melt. His tiny body so full of power and pride, like a miniature tiger pouncing on me, purring and licking me with a disregard for all but passion. I loved the way he smelled. You know, smell is very important. And the way a person smells changes. So you must keep him close and keep sniffing and scratching. Meow!

I actually like to tell myself it is he who blew it, not me. I am a true-blue baby dago. I would have walked him to his grave one diaper change at a time, attending to his every whim—lover, friend, secretary, and housekeeper, not to mention a superior stepmom all in one touch of the hand. Yes, he can be with others, but none as true as me. That you can take to the Hall of Music. Note to God: Dear Lord, I wish Mr. Valli would see what is in my soul and the genuineness of my emotions. Note to self: Move on little lady, you deserve someone who loves you.

Imagine the euphoria of Christmas, New Year's Eve, your birthday, and the Fourth of July all rolled into one. That's how I felt. My man wanted me. I couldn't wait to see him.

Our contact with one another went through the ups and downs of our lives. It is like a family; we are always around, and even if we don't hook up this trip, it's because one of us has personal business to address. When you are involved on some level for over thirty years—from no cell phones or computers to social media—it just evolves.

When I arrived at the venue, the name of which I don't remember anymore and it really doesn't matter, Frankie's guys were around his bus, doing their jobs. Frankie had told them to stay away from me, but a couple of them approached me anyway. Who does that to their boss? We had a romantic night once again, with five-star treatment, and a few people asked me for my autograph. I just chucked and said, "Oh, I think you really want Frankie's." Still, I was thrilled from the top of my head to the tips of my red-polished toes. We had two wonderful days and nights together before my world crashed.

We were upstairs, my heart thundering in my chest like a herd of runaway cattle, when Frankie was called away.

"I'll be right back," he said.

I smiled and hugged him, slipping off my heels to freshen up for bed.

It had been a long time, and things were going as I had hoped. "Pinch me," I said to myself, looking in the mirror. "It's true. I am free from Youngstown. I'm so ready for this." With a stagehand following him into the suite, Frankie walked back into the room and stared at me with the killer eyes of a great white shark. The butterflies in my heart fell into my stomach. He gave me an "I don't need this shit from anyone" look. Then he spoke, "Your husband is outside!"

At first I thought it might be Marc. Billy and I weren't married, so it never crossed my mind that he had driven all day from Hubbard, Ohio.

"Marc?" I said. "He and I—"

"Billy," said the stagehand.

You might as well put a stake through my heart and wrap garlic on my head. The life I had dreamed burst into flames. I still get upset about what Billy did. He was just a kid at the time, probably eighteen, but he lied. I wanted to smack him on his little head. We weren't married. I was just living with him. Yes, I cared, but marriage was the furthest thing from my mind at that time. He pretended to be my husband. He was saying things only a husband should say, not a boyfriend. Once again, someone tries to put me in a birdcage, and I don't like it. I need the cage door open, and I always fly home unless I'm forced to flee. He was forcing me to dislike and disrespect him on many levels. As a Sagittarius, it is a pet peeve to find lies in love. Lies are a virus that infects the core of where my blood once gushed, leading me to a man's bed. Once that happens, no amount of Bacardi or porn will rekindle the juices that once flowed joining me to him.

It's the little things that make the knife pierce through the heart and make passion leave, more like little cuts, I suppose, that eventually make a hole that can't be repaired. I think that is where I started to fall out of love with Billy. He crossed the line. I didn't go to his job and make up stories to pick up his check early. Seriously!

I had waited years for this chance. The fighter in me had worked hard for what I wanted: Frankie. A woman with a passion to get her man can fuel a rocket to the moon and back. And I just lost mine.

In that moment, I knew Frankie and I were done. With one stupid action, Billy ended everything I had ever lived for. Everything that I planned for. Everything that I worked for. All the work, the years invested in grooming myself to be the kind of female ready to tackle a star like Mr. Valli.

"It's time to go downstairs," Frankie said. "Then I think I'll get you a flight home."

I tried to speak, but he wouldn't let me give my side of the story.

Things got very uncomfortable backstage, like entering a funeral parlor with no one there but you, the corpse, and a cool breeze that swirled with remnants of a lovely scent from wilting flowers. Billy had apparently tried to get in, but wasn't allowed. I guess he turned around and drove back to Hubbard. I didn't want to know. I didn't care at that moment. Later, when I got over the shock of what happened, I felt a little guilty that he drove back by himself. But just a little. Part of me felt he deserved that lonely trip because of what he did to me and my Frankie.

I don't remember much more of that night. The thundering cattle became the wail of a massive slaughter. I didn't see Frankie after the show. We didn't even talk. He wanted me gone. And I was just a dim memory by the next morning. I really wanted to talk. I wanted him to hear my side of the story. He's not much into deep-meaning dialogue though, at least not with me. I wanted to convince Frankie that Billy had lied. The last look I remember on Frankie's face told me that it was best to just keep my little mouth shut.

It was a flight that seemed to never end, and I cried all the way. I'm sure passengers thought someone had died. For me, someone did! When I arrived at our tiny, old-fashioned apartment in Hubbard, Ohio, I saw a Billy with red, swollen eyes. He had driven my sports car to Chicago and back to fight against an icon to win my heart. Most women would fall madly crazy in love with a guy who would drive four hundred miles to profess his love. I was pissed. He sat on the couch, smoking a cigarette and holding my dog, while I carried my bags upstairs. He surprised me, though, when he thanked me for coming home.

I didn't say anything. What was I supposed to do? I had to come home. Frankie wouldn't have me at that point. Billy saw to that. Another one who didn't like to talk, Billy was quiet about the entire incident. I fumed when he pretended nothing happened. Is that a man thing? Why don't men like to talk! We girls want to talk and talk and talk until nothing else will spill out of our souls.

"I'm glad you're back. I missed you," he whispered.

I stomped away and resounded in the sternest voice I could muster without screaming, "We aren't married."

He nodded and replied almost inaudibly, "I guess to me we're married."

That stopped me. I was immediately frozen, unable to move forward or background with the present staring me squarely in the face. What could I say to that? Absolutely nothing. I let that reality sink in while he wrapped his arms around me as I stood like a cold, lifeless mannequin. Then I slipped out of one of my designer dresses and hung it in the little closet in the country-styled bedroom, knowing that I would never wear it again. I don't think I ever put that clingy, seductive number on again. I probably gave it away to someone who would wear it to places I only hoped to saunter through, dazzling each person with a warm, welcoming smile.

Billy knew he lied. He knew what I wanted. But Billy wanted me. I had to give him that much. I respect a man who loves me so much that he's willing to do whatever it takes to fight for "us" even when I'm on the opposing side with the enemy. I am either a sucker or a survivor; to this day, I'm not sure which.

Not long after I got home, the phone rang. Billy answered and then, with a scowl on his face, he rolled those big baby-blue eyes while he cringed as he handed me the receiver. It was Frankie. I gulped. I couldn't utter a sound. To this very day, I wonder how this little dago wielded such power over me to shock me into silence. He didn't say much, but I remember the words to this day: "I'm glad you made it home." I could feel my heart momentarily putting itself back together, surging with excitement and possibility. And then it shattered again into a zillion pieces, cutting every atom in my being. "Work on your marriage with your husband. Maybe we will talk again soon."

I wanted to beg and plead for one more chance, just one

more. Something stopped me cold in my tracks. Whether it was pride or wisdom, I still cannot decipher. I only know I had grown to know as a woman that when a man for whatever reason makes up his mind that a particular woman is not for him, it's a done deal. It's odd, this thing called love. The entire process of falling in and out of love is a rather magical recipe that can never be duplicated. A woman could fall for her guy because he has the cutest giggle. A man could decide to delete a phone number because he couldn't stand the sound of his date munching potato chips during a movie. It's weird. It lacks logic. This emotional drama totally ruined my chance for a life with Frankie. It was like the giant Hollywood sign flashed lights to the entire universe and it shouted, "Billy Kirkwood Screws Up April Gatta's Life."

I knew Frankie wouldn't ever reach out to me again, and he never did. I always got the impression that once he thought you deceived or screwed him, Mr. Valli was the sort of fellow who was never going to be open to letting it happen again. When we connected years later, it was me who pursued him. Billy also knew Frankie wouldn't call, and why would he! He could have anyone, anywhere, anytime without any hassle or bullshit. For Billy I think it was a huge sick kind of victory for him to overthrow Frankie from his little kingdom. Billy fought and conquered Frankie, winning his prize and bringing her back to their quaint cottage. Billy could now proceed with building his world, with me as its center.

Still, I could not fathom for the life of me how quickly this all went down. I didn't even have the opportunity to defend or explain myself. It's like watching someone get killed on the highway. They are zooming along in their car, with plans for their day, and boom—a truck rolls over the median strip and crashes into them, and they're dead on the spot, all in the blink of an eye. Both men were at fault, and both should have been cited for reckless abuse of a soul on the highway of life.

Billy was guilty for the obvious reasons of ruthless deception and abandonment of the truth, and Frankie believed a punk kid he didn't know over me—the little girl he had a friendship with since she was barely eight years old. How could he not trust me and value my dedication to him to always be forthright and up-front about every aspect and detail of my world? I was always truthful and true-blue.

Being honest was, and still is, something that I pride myself in, especially with the men in my life. I can be virtuous to a painful fault. Add an Italian personality to a Sagittarius with a Scorpio rising, and it's definite fire. Sometimes I even inflict pain with words that I probably should never let come out of my mouth. That doesn't happen often now. I've learned to control my tongue, because it's true that words are sharper than any sword or knife. As all wise women know who rule their kingdom with dignity and grace, you gather more flies with honey than vinegar.

I gently placed the phone back on the hook as though to pretend the conversation never happened. In reality, a thousand thoughts pulsated through my entire body in bipolar kind of schizophrenia. I wanted to lash out at Billy, but I didn't. I didn't have the energy, to be quite frank. I was mentally, emotionally, and physically exhausted. Instead, I quickly marched into the bathroom and soaked in a hot bubble bath of Estée Lauder oils. I cried into a washcloth with Lovie sitting beside the tub, wagging her tail. After soaking until my skin was pink and wrinkled, I put on my pj's, snuck out, and crawled into bed alone. I held Lovie tight, praying I would wake up to yesterday and this could be stopped as tears lulled me to sleep.

I got Billy back for his stunt. Moi, vindictive? That's the Scorpio rising in me, another negative! I shut him out. I didn't speak to him for days. I learned from Frankie himself that silence is more deadly than words, and at this point, it was the vengeance against Billy I could conjure up. He tried to get me to talk, but I wouldn't. I walked away or picked up a magazine and pretended to read. I wanted to move out, throw pictures of us out the window, something that would have allowed me to blow off some steam. Instead, I did nothing. I had nowhere to go. So I stayed and slept.

I sleep when I'm distraught. That's my MO. I don't talk on the phone, don't watch TV or eat. I guess you could say I'm the queen of sleep. I've done a lot of sleeping in my life, without the use of pills. I just shut down. I find it's less expensive than mall therapy and less detrimental to my mental health than drinking and partying. And let's face, most people don't really want to hear sob stories. After five minutes, it's like, "OK enough, time to move on. Buck up and get back on board."

I slept a lot after returning from Chicago. I only left the bedroom to cook and work. It took weeks for me to warm up to Billy again. One night he came home with his hands in his pockets. I heard this strange squeak. He pulled out two yellow baby ducks. I gushed, showering him with kisses. I always had ducks as a little girl, and he remembered. It was charming. How could I resist? I couldn't, and I kissed him some more.

Another endearing moment was when Billy drove me to work during a bad storm early on a gray Youngstown morning. Working in an office, I had always dressed for success. That morning I donned a beautiful pair of red patent leather heels. When we arrived at Equitable Assurance, with a staff of all women, he ran around the car, opened the door, and carried me into my office so I didn't get my feet wet. I had forgotten the incident until I saw Joannie, an adorable coworker of mine, while in the midst of writing this book, and she recalled the entire scene as if from a romance novel. I was shocked that I'd forgotten until then. It's odd what people recall and what they let slip out of their lives, rewriting events as they go to give them a sense of peace to somehow justify their actions.

Humble beginnings on a chicken farm in the Midwest. The Dream Team (Left to right) Mom, Grandma, Ginny, Grandpa, Aunt Rosie.

Ralph Joseph Gatta, my Dad, quiet unassuming expressing himself with music. His message: Family first, money ain't bad either, and always do it with class!

Beverly Jean Kata marries Ralph Joseph Gatta. The farm house nestled in the woods where I grew up.

My secluded childhood in Trumbul County, Liberty Township, Ohio. Gravel driveway, pets galore, and time to wander in the silence of nature.

The second moment a six-year-old little girl met the man of her dreams, Frankie Valli. Sandusky, Ohio, Cedar Point with the infamous banner and hat.

The famous, Stambaugh Auditorium, Youngstown, Ohio with Aunt Ginny and classmate, Barbara Dunning.

The meeting place: Stambaugh with cousin, Terie Lee Kata and Barbara with Tommy DeVito. The velvet suit made in the image of Frankie's and the hat that became my backstage pass.

Competition and winning were a way of life for me. From Junior Miss to winning the crown of Miss Ohio Teenager, 1975.

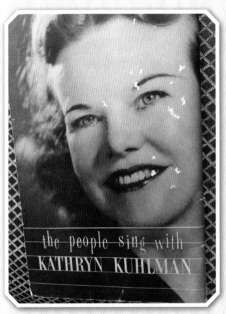

Synchronicity rears its head as each Sunday, Kathryn Kuhlman conducted church services where I joined the choir and youth group.

I continued to see Frankie Valli at every opportunity with my family in attendance as well. Back stage, green rooms, radio interviews were now part of my life with this adorable mega star.

Joey Long poses for a picture.

Back home a simple refrigerator represents the lifestyle of a little girl, her family, and prayers.

Dale Crain, the first boyfriend, loses me only to the gravitational pull to Frankie and the world awaiting.

The Christian Grey of my youth in terms of showing me a larger more sophisticated life in South Florida, Chicago style, but still within the safety net of Youngstown, Ohio. Out of all of the men, he loved me most.

Mom and step-dad, Leslie Thomas. This is the picture at my wedding. It was a sad day for my mom, as she was right, I was too young to marry anyone. Aunt Ginny did most of the planning!

Billy, the musician, the flirt, the born-again kid who was made to love me. The famous car that drove Billy to Chicago to win my love.

It's back to the Holiday Inn circuit with another musician. A trumpet player like no other; church grown with a four-year music scholarship and couldn't read a sheet of symphonic music. We met at Dana School of Music in a play, Kismet. The rest is history.

Northside Hospital, Youngstown, Ohio. Billy and April Kirkwood bring their first child into the world, Dana Nicole Kirkwood, with proud grandparents, Grandma Bevy and Papa Les.

At age 51, better late than never and ready now.

In Ohio once again, but by now, I'll travel to Pennsylvania, New York, Illinois and Michigan to be with him. Reunited with my first love, cemented into my DNA, under my skin, forever feeling an odd sense of comfort when I'm with him.

Sitting backstage; my favorite thing about Frankie is the way he wrapped his arms around me. He's strong even with a small stature, there's a definite power. It wasn't sex to me; it was more, much more. I don't think he ever knew. I know I can never get back what I gave to him.

The man I love most in the world, my son, Grant in the movie, Gods and Generals. Grant was inappropriately given the title, "man of the house." Add to that losing his dad, and the struggles of growing up has made him into a magnificent source of inspiration for all who know him.

My Frankie look alike twin soul shows up quite unannounced right under my nose in my back yard....Ytown, the Italian stop off from NYC. He had me at Hello.....like Frankie, he gave it little thought. He had three children and a wife at home as well as being a big fish in a small town.

Dana goes off to the University of Miami, Coral Gables, Florida. I soon move down to avoid the chaos of Ron's lies and experience a new life.

Years after being his mistress, Ralph divorces and movies immediately in with me into the South Florida home where I had been well kept for several years. I take hope praying that dreams do come true. Finally I will get it right and be an appropriate married Italian lady with children and grandchildren to love.

The soul survivor of my dream team, Aunt Ginny and the famous partner in crime, Uncle Chuck. These two people are my salvation. If the tears I've cried in their arms were gold, they would be millionaires. They reside in Florida half the year with grandkids in Boca and spend summers in Chicago with more grandchildren. Family is important to them!

Mr. and Mrs. Curtis Nystrom, alumni of University of Miami. Dana has her master's degree and is in education and Curtis is in music management where they reside with their yorkie, Jerry, in Brooklyn, New York.

Where Dana is weak, Grant is strong....they provide so much in my life and I enjoy each precious moment in their presence. Grant presently is single and resides in the Delray area near his Mommy, like a good son.

The book mysteriously found days after my Mom's passing. It is the blessed assurance that one day my dream team will be united in love and light.

I must have wanted to forget the wonderful moments to validate my divorce. Pitiful, isn't it! We actually are the directors of our own lives, even when it is written with flaws and distortions.

Even when I was furious with him, Billy knew how to make me laugh like a little girl. He would put on my robe, dance around, and make me giggle so hard I would almost pee my pants. I love to laugh. He made me crack up a lot back then, something I needed. Something I still need. A man who can make you chuckle is one who can take you through the ups and downs in life and still see the silver lining around the moon. Billy did that at first.

Billy and I were together for a total of seventeen years. We were barely in our twenties. I had our first child, Dana Nicole, when I was twenty-six. Billy was twenty-three.

And so for a while, I didn't think much about being the next Mrs. Frankie Valli. Instead I focused on my relationship with Billy. Sure, I thought about Frankie from time to time. I'd think of our times together when I heard one of his songs on the radio or I'd see a place that we had visited when we were together. My children knew his songs by heart as early as three years of age. But that's as far as it went. I quit pining for him during every waking moment. I finally got to the place that we all need to get—I wouldn't sink my relationship with Billy, knowing that Frankie's boat or yacht had sailed. I'm blond, but I'm not stupid.

One might think that I settled. Maybe I did. I was home in Youngstown, Ohio, near my dream team. My grandma paid for me to go to graduate school. My mom showered the kids like we were millionaires. And my aunt Ginny and uncle Chuck were there to create more fond memories with. We were all just having "normal" Midwest fun in the '80s. For the first time I finally felt content in my love life even when my mom butted in, we were doing OK. More than OK, I see looking back.

But—and there's always a but, right?—that emotion would soon rear its ugly head again.

CHAPTER 6

Tell It to the Rain

Ladies, when we don't get the man we set our intentions on, we do some pretty crazy things, right? I know I have. I won't specifically admit to what I've done on the list below, but here are some vandalizing acts of romantic desperation that ladies from the past and present have been known to do in the name of innocent passion and devotion:

- Leaving notes on their car or door
- Texting or calling over and over
- Taking the same classes in college
- Hanging out with their friends
- Dancing around the oak tree naked, chanting weird incantations, sprinkling incense
- Reading every how-to book about love and romance
- Buying crotchless panties and handcuffs
- Driving past their place even though it's fifteen minutes out of the way to work
- Checking their cell phone history
- Adding a GPS tracker to the bottom of their car

This bizarre kind of drama causes even the most determined women to eventually ask one haunting question: "When do I give up?" We lose hours of sleep, tossing and turning, trying to figure out "How long do I keep trying" or "Am I wasting my time?" The decision to finally close the door and turn your back on your own goals takes great courage. And men, just for the record, you are a goal if we think that you are the catch of our lifetime. Then, of course, if our biological clock is ticking every night you become even a better prize. It sucks because there are no clear-cut, hard rules for dating and waiting in this new age of feminine empowerment. However, I found one fact that rings true: when you have to do most of the work, it's not true love. If you have to convince, trick, or seduce anyone to desire and commit to you, there's a chance that you are headed for a stay at the Heartbreak Hotel. See, through all the social media, hype, and immediate messaging, there is one secret that your grandma knew that we obviously don't. Yes, it's no random accident that these old-fashioned ladies didn't get divorced and their husbands scampered home night after night, year after year, through both the up and the down years of wedding bliss. She knew how to keep her man, even after matrimony, and it wasn't because she was stunning, wealthy, or even a superwoman. This is the secret I didn't realize and maybe you don't know either: A woman never chases a man. Never, never, never. Men by instinct are hunters. I hate it to acknowledge this truth, but I have grown to accept the possibility that it is a vital ingredient in their DNA and is not disappearing anytime soon. This, ladies, is the beginning of growing up into a wise woman, knowing what you can and can't change and accommodating. It's in all men's DNA to spread their seed so the world can survive, and we as ladies need to learn to navigate around this little piece of biology. Ever wonder what he does now that he has you in that pumpkin shell with his name on the deed? Well, lovely ladies,

I know; he's out hunting someone else. So how do you keep him wanting you in his arms above any other contender for the position of his one and only? Make sure you never, never, never chase him on any level. My grandma would never call her husband at his mother's house. She was too busy enjoying her life, or at least that's what she led him to believe. He began to wonder what she was up to out and about all day, and he called her, brought in a rose from the garden, and was home on time for supper for over fifty years, come hell or high water.

This leads me to the next most tormented questions we gals ask ourselves: When do we have sex with him? How long are we supposed to wait? Will he think I'm a whore if I do him like a stripper? Will he leave if I don't do it, labeling me a tease? Will having sex seal the deal?

We all know that guys are horndogs and think about sex like every few minutes. We know that most men are just darling boys in grown-up clothes, with porn smuggled away somewhere. But it used to be so much easier for women to circumvent men who always wanted it anytime, anyplace, twenty-four seven. In the past there was an unspoken code that the third date was the do-it-or-don't-do-it date. This was the turning point in the relationship and let all parties involved know whether they were going to the next level. Sex took it to the next level. No sex kept it on the same playing field, sliding into the friend zone.

Today the rules have been modified greatly, or do we have protocols about intimacy at all? Oral sex is like shaking hands and having sex on a first or second date is not regarded as a big deal. I realize I'm old, but I still wonder what guys really think about not having to work for it. What kind of passionate dance is in that? I, for one, enjoy a little cat and mouse. It makes the romp so much more exciting when I've visualized fifty shades of erotica for a while before we go meet body-to-body, naked, with all our flaws, staring into each other's eyes.

The other sappy mystery is pondering whether having sex with a guy is even a guarantee that he's going to call tomorrow. Let me clue you in: spreading your legs doesn't guarantee anything. If it were that easy, every hooker in Hollywood would be living in a mansion in Calabasas right now next to Frankie Valli. The old adage from Andrew Carnegie is true: "Anything in life worth having is worth working for." Consider this: the big bang theory is based on the concept of a universal soul energy that became bored having absolutely everything handed to it. Insane, right? The group consciousness requested to its all-giving god to be given the gift of creating as he/she has done. We collectively wanted to derive the same bliss and joy in that process as he/she does. In short, we wanted to have to put forth a little effort and work to get all the good things God previously gave us immediately just for showing up. Kind of sucks, right? But I do get it. For example, I prefer getting a promotion when I know I justly deserve it, not because I'm dating the president's son.

Now, I understand that some women make it a game to bed as many guys as possible. That's a separate issue. For these women, sex is a sport, much like football is a sport for guys. With all sports, you can lose your contract and be replaced by a younger, quicker team player.

It's a dilemma, I agree, and it comes up with each new relationship as the same old bump in the road. How many of us, including me, have dialed in a dizzy frenzy the 1-900 psychic hotline or visited an intuitive, or as they were once called, a fortune-teller? I'm willing to bet that on any night of the week, you'll have at least two or three women you know phoning in, asking, "Is he going to call? Is he cheating on me? Does he love me? What should I do? Is he the one? Should I get married? Should I get a divorce? Should I cheat?" That has to be one of lowest moments for any woman who foolishly ascertains she's in total control of her own life. I admit that I've dialed it up more than a time or two. In fact, I've gotten really astute in doing tarot cards myself. I think we can all agree that when in love, we become obsessed and mad out of control, tipping the envelope of "gone certifiably nuts" to get our man.

Let's revisit my screw-ups. I picked the wrong guy again when I met Billy Kirkwood, two years my junior. I was just turning twenty-two.

Billy had a four-year music scholarship to Youngstown State. He played trumpet but could not read sheet music. He learned in the church and a Polish polka band. He was accepted into the United States Youth Orchestra and traveled abroad at the age of fifteen. He played from his gut and was fabulous. However, Billy had no ambition to study. Once again, I get this speech from the dean of music, warning me that this young man is not the best for a girl like me. For as many times as people have tried to caution me about the wrong guy, it would be nice if someone would recommend the right one for once. So Mr. Kirkwood spent most of his time playing pool and chatting with girls on campus. I was in the process of getting divorced from Marc after getting scared senseless from his gambling. I mean, who gets a toy gun out to protect himself. Even I know better!

After Marc Pagano, I searched for the common elements that were at my core. I guess I was scared of associating and admiring a lifestyle of greed and corruptness. That aversion didn't last forever, sorry to say. I enjoyed the safety of Billy because he was more like me than I cared to admit to him, his family, but mostly myself. We both were raised in the church, and that was the string that kept us drawn to each other even when everything else was falling apart. I was totally, totally over the top attracted to Billy, but I'm still not sure why. Little did I know that he wasn't that smart. He had no money and was very poor. His family never accepted me. They were deacons of the church, led by rules, regulations, and judgment.

As a free spirit, I loathed those qualities most from humanity. They would have fit in perfectly at Oral Roberts University had they been able to afford it. They kicked Billy out of the house for dating such a sinful married woman; my divorce was not final. My family, as dysfunctional as they could be at times, would not let someone live homeless on the street and stepped in to help me and my new beau. He had these two huge sea-blue eyes, was six feet two inches, and had a slender body that could grace the cover of *GQ*.

Some of my mom's friends, an elderly couple who attended Kathryn Kuhlman Ministry with us at Stambaugh Auditorium for years, left their house to my family after they passed away. The little home rested one street behind ours in the woods, where it sat abandoned for years, looking worn and shabby. We managed to put a bed in there, and that was about it. Like most young couples in love, having a bed and a room was all Billy and I needed.

We had steamy romps everywhere. There was an animal knowing between us that required little verbal communication and was formed and demonstrated in physical gratification, as though we were old friends worshipping each other after a long time of separation. And it was also a time of celebrating our youth and freedom, experimenting together in an age of middle-class monetary spending. He was in a band called Natural Force, with a little midget guy who sang and played the saxophone and a full-piece brass section, with Billy being the token white musician. This all-black funk band in the '80s played the Holiday Inn circuit, with a full entourage of wives, girlfriends, dope, and Jheri curl. Billy really was a church-grown, gifted trumpet player. I enjoyed traveling in our beat-up car, being part of this simple, uncomplicated lifestyle. I felt like I was on a permanent vacation from marriage, school, and responsibility. Everyone would say, "Billy has chops." He truly did. Billy had a bit of swagger on stage, and the girls loved him. Mr. Kirkwood was tall, with wavy brown hair, giant blue eyes, and hips that Elvis would envy. The guys even put me to work and taught me how to run the light board. If Billy looked at a girl, I would momentarily turn the lights off on him. It was just for a second, and I always got the greatest laughs from it. If you would label me anything, I'd rather be compared to a mischievous wood sprite enjoying going left when everyone is taking a turn to the right. Like me, I think Billy was groomed to be on stage. My family supported him as much as they could by attending shows often. Aunt Ginny, Uncle Chuck, my cousin Kathy, and I were the "white folk" at the shows. We learned how to "get jiggy wit' it" and stay up to the wee hours, throwing down with the best of them.

Playing the nightclub circuit—with the live bands and floor shows made popular by the movie *Saturday Night Fever*—was the pinnacle for bands like the one Billy played in. It seemed we were booked away most weekends. In the '70s and '80s, everyone looked the part. For women, that meant Farrah Fawcett hair, a minidress or one-piece jumpsuit, hoop earrings, bangle bracelets, lip gloss, and high heels to dance in. For guys, it was long hair, bell-bottoms, and big-collared shirts.

Remember, before this time in American history, the middle class didn't have the freedom to fly on airplanes, party like it was the end of the century, own Corvettes, and shop at high-end boutiques. This was an era of unlimited resources and experimentation for the normal Joe. Well, we really didn't do anything much, looking back on it. Our '70s and '80s wild experimentation consisted of whether we could stay out and still get to work on time each morning. We always did.

All musicians know that you take jobs wherever you can. My aunt Ginny and uncle Chuck came to this dive that I remember was particularly rough. Bouncers required every-one to check whatever they were packing at the door. If you had a gun, you couldn't get in if you didn't check it. My mom and grandma would have died if they knew that. Uncle Chuck carried most of the time, so I felt safe with him and Aunt Ginny. My uncle was a looker, too. Notice a pattern here? It seemed that I only knew and hung out with good-looking men.

Chuck was tall, handsome, and always up for any action we threw his way. He loved to tell stories over and over and over. Still, he likes to read the newspaper out loud, so we are all educated. And, of course, he had commentary on all news-worthy pieces, so we were bound and tied to sit and discuss. Today, as the truth has become easier to spit out, we just call him "Chuck Talk a Lot." I do it because Big Chuck has put up with all of us girls, and when push comes to shove, he would do just about anything for any one of us. You had to give the guy credit for taking Aunt Ginny's niece on as one of his own. One time in the '70s, I talked him into taking us to a cool bar in New York City because a handsome guy on the plane told me to make sure I check it out. Aunt Ginny and I stormed in, going full throttle to the back near the music, with Uncle Chuck trailing close behind, trying to stop us. Turns out, I had talked him into taking us to a gay bar. In the '70s, being in a gay bar was much, much more exclusive and secluded than it is today. A lot of heads turned our way that night before Chuck was politely asked to have us, not him, leave.

During the summer of 1980, Billy and I moved in togeth-er on a cute little side street in Hubbard, Ohio, in the same suburb where I much later became a middle school guid-ance counselor. My mother wasn't thrilled at losing me again and put on the brakes as much as she could. The Queen Bee proclaimed, "If you want this, you have to come up with the money." So I did what any woman in love would do; I sold my stunning little pale-blue Triumph and set us up in a little upstairs apartment, twenty steps above the Bar family, who we grew to love very much. The husband, Danny, died a year before Billy in a tragic motorcycle accident.

The place above the Bars was just five small rooms in their house with white siding. We didn't have much space to get away from each other when we were mad. But it was just about perfect when things were going well. We couldn't afford to lavishly decorate it.

I came home one night after work to find Billy with a ring on our little kitchen table. He told me that we're getting married the next day or I could get out. Mind you, this is the very apartment I sold my stunning little blue Triumph to furnish. I don't think we had ever talked about getting married. But when he came to me with the ring, the plans, and his authoritative words, I threw out all the warnings of my heart and packed an overnight bag.

We drove through a winter storm from Youngstown to Norfolk, Virginia, at the time the marriage capital of the world, where it was open twenty-four hours a day. But nothing was open. Billy found a justice of the peace in an old house down a dirt road. He looked like a homeless man, but he was kind and invited us to his house where we were married in his living room. Billy had his heart set on this, and he did it in spite of the odds against it happening. So next thing I knew, in a pair of blue jeans and a tight cream cashmere sweater with cream cowboy boots, I became Mrs. William Raymond Kirkwood.

After that, we did what I think is one of the strangest things I'd ever done—we left the judge's house and found a CVS, where we silently shopped separately for cards and toiletries. I don't remember what kind of card I bought my new husband. Or what he bought me. It just sticks out in my mind that moments after we got married, we split up to shop. Most couples cling to each other, but not us. I think we were both in shock.

We drove home in total white-out snow, falling so quickly snowplows couldn't even keep up. Billy fought the car numerous times to keep us from sliding off the side of the road. I wondered if this storm was a sign of doom and gloom ahead. I look back at our relationship, and it seems that something always hindered us—the weather, our parents, our jobs, something. It took us forever to get home, to get started, to begin. We didn't talk much since he needed to concentrate on the roads, his beautiful trumpet hands gripping the steering wheel. I didn't want to get blamed for causing a wreck, although Billy wasn't the kind of guy who would blame me for anything. So I sat in the passenger seat of our little Chevy and did what I did when stressed or confused—I slipped into autopilot.

Billy was nineteen and I was twenty-two, so we set up housekeeping, beginning our new life together as man and wife, saving to buy a home. I had my eye on my aunt and uncle's three-story turn-of-the-century big white farmhouse. It had a four-car garage and a great yard, and our eventual babies could attend the Liberty School System as my entire family did. For a starter place, I think it was country-chic charming. We enjoyed working together to make it a home, going to garage sales, getting furniture from my mom, and making the best use of layaway for high-end items.

Billy and I both had jobs to get enough money for the deposit we needed. He worked days at the Ohio Bureau of Unemployment, and I was at Equitable Assurance. I also went to college, and he played in a band at night. We saved money, got great credit, and eventually bought it. The house was so large that it had been converted into two apartments above us, which paid the mortgage. Soon Billy and I were landscaping and Billy had a gift with home construction.

Four years into the marriage, Billy announced that it was time I had a baby. Again, he got this idea and was relentless, and I fell prey to this new passion. But at twenty-six, I was ready, and I got pregnant in about one second. I gave birth to our daughter Dana in July of 1984. She was the love of our lives. Her blond hair and hazel eyes melted the hearts of anyone who met her. The sun seemed to always shine around her.

I made the mistake of changing drastically after I had Baby Dana, my little Leo with Gemini rising. I reinvented myself from the simple little farm girl to the lady who dove into the world of the upper-middle class, demanding I give the very best to Miss Dana. It's as though a light switch flipped on. Now, in retrospect, I wonder if that's where I went off course. The Jewish Community Center was a must for preschool, as was Logan Swim Club and Ballet Western Reserve. I clothed Dana in semi-designer wear for toddlers—pricey Zoodles outfits with matching socks and bows. I made sure that Dana had them all. Ironically, the creators lived in our community, making it a staple in every little girl's wardrobe. Come to think of it, perhaps this is the instant I came alive. I was restless, a new mother living within a budget from paycheck to paycheck, alone most of the time in a big house. I accidentally happened upon a video on the chakras, Shirley MacLaine, and closed-eye meditation. Something happened to me. Call it salvation, an awakening, the aha moment—my life became clearer than it ever has, illuminating the beauty of Eastern and Western spirituality and the awareness of the feminine goddess within my being. My life since then has been nothing less than an adventure with myself, learning to "be," following my heart's calling, wishing harm on no one, with a new desire to become of service to every human being. I didn't know at the time how very much I had to experience, the lessons both joyful and sorrowful. The challenges between my ego, consciousness, and soul's knowing continued; now I am just more aware when I screwed up.

This zest for the best spilled over to other aspects of our lives. As a little girl growing up, I recall the moment I realized I wasn't from a rich family. A girl by the name of Susan came to my house. As I ushered her into my bedroom, so proud of my canopy bed and white princess phone, she declared in a noble, condescending tone, "It's not that nice, and your street isn't that great." It never occurred to me that my room wasn't as nice as anyone else's. It never occurred to me we were not rich. I always felt rich and wonderfully blessed. That moment stuck with me for the rest of my life. A silly little girl with a nasty attitude affected such emotion and still rolled her eyes in my head, reminding me that I needed to protect Dana from ever feeling the way I did at that moment.

All of a sudden, with Baby Dana, I decided our old car wouldn't do. On a snowy day, with income tax check in hand, I sent Billy out to purchase a car of taste for our princess. He came in eight hours later, tattered from the weather, with a beautiful Audi. He knew social status had become important to me, and I think my high standards were part of what he loved about me and hated about me all in one sigh. I have always set the standards very high for myself, and those I loved were part of the vision I had for what I thought at the time was a fulfilling life. I had quit my job to be a stay-at-home mom only four days after returning from maternity leave, because the sitter told me, "Dana no longer likes peaches. Please bring pears next week for her lunch." I realized I didn't know what my baby liked to eat. That did it for me. I quit my job. I didn't even talk with Billy about it. He was already an ironworker, thanks to my stepdad, providing us with a very impressive income. A weekend of overtime could easily bring in $2,000 in the '80s. Despite the great money, Billy started his own company, ALK Erections. The company put covers on gas stations for self-service. They are a staple now at every station.

He began to travel for weeks on end, and I didn't mind. I created my own private world as a mommy, and I loved it. Every day was a celebration of life. Jell-O molds, paint for the tub, decorating for each season, and having fun together. My favorite job is being a mom. I have found no greater satisfaction.

I found out that Billy was a serial cheater from my little brother who often worked with the guys in the summer. I was stunned. I hated him for it. I wanted him for it. I wanted to run over him and then have wild sex with him and make more babies. I wanted him to hurt. I wanted him to feel my pain. We were perfect for each other; I realized that too late. Was I lost in Frankie again? Was I in the dream of Hollywood and rock and roll, or was it more? I screwed it up big time.

He was six foot two, with an ironworker's body, built like a brick. His biggest asset, though, was his charisma. Billy could charm the pants off a woman so that they vowed their monogamy until death.

It wasn't a big surprise when we drifted apart. I continued to work on my master's. I joined the Junior League, was on the board of Ballet Western Reserve, and was a teacher at the Jewish Community Center. I created a world for my family, and unfortunately Billy didn't want to join me, nor was he comfortable in that arena. He became an outcast due to his own choosing. Dana was in preschool and was socially growing with friends, day camps, and places that kept me busy and happy.

Believe it or not, despite his affairs, I still wanted Billy. I know that sounds strange, but he was my husband, and I didn't want to divorce again. We were working through things when I got pregnant again. I gave birth to Grant three and a half years after Dana. He was adorable. I know all mothers say that about their kids. I knew exactly what he was going to look like since the moment I conceived. He was born with gorgeous brown hair and deep, dark eyes. He was adorable.

Although Grant wasn't a preemie, he wouldn't breathe on his own. A league of specialists put him in an incubator for three weeks. I had thought that these were the three toughest weeks my life. Any mother who has seen their child suffer will understand. My baby was so tiny, and I couldn't do anything for him. My in-laws rallied and came in with their pastor, praying and helping me keep the house in order. Dana was with my mom and continued to attend the Jewish Community Center preschool program.

But there was Grant. Battling this was the first of what would be many challenges to come. Nothing seemed to help him. All of a sudden, when he was ready, he unexplainably started to breathe on his own. But soon after, Grantster developed colic, then constipation, and the list grew after that. His first words were "help me." I admit, we conceived Grant under the stress of emotional pain, hoping this save-the-marriage baby would heal the past by creating a new future. It also seems Grant Charles (after Uncle Chuck) was born under some strange stars January 19, 1988. I feel guilty for this because I picked the date for my C-section, not realizing I picked the day that both Edgar Allan Poe and Janis Joplin were born. After studying natal astrological charts some time later, I learned that could be disastrous. My grandma is probably saying from heaven, "April, you're going to hell in a basket." But I believe all studies bear some fruit, and exploration leads to greater self-understanding. "Three Hail Marys for that one."

My mother, brought up evangelical, yelled coldly at Billy, "This baby is sick and is scorned by the sins of his father." Of course that is not true. Anyone who has studied Christianity or is a true believer knows that God doesn't punish people in that manner. Billy and I were hurt, but that comment is the kind we came to expect from my mother, and just as quickly as she said it, she denied ever saying such an evil thing. She had no filter between her mind and her mouth, and I sensed a lack of remorse for saying it. If there was ever an attempt to discuss a negative comment, she brushed it off as casually as Scarlett O'Hara shooed off Rhett Butler's attempt to woo her.

Grant's hardships have plagued him all his life, and me as well. How can any mother be content when one of her baby birds isn't soaring with the rest of the flock? For example, during parades, he would patiently wait for candy and balloons, lined up with friends and neighbors, only to discover there were none left by the time they got to him. All of his birthday parties were snuffed out by gigantic snowstorms. These are the kinds of thing that, unfortunately, resembled more of a pattern than an isolated catastrophe.

During Grant's formative years, Billy and I were growing apart, so Grant leaned on me. He suffered from my divorce in many ways. Although we all reconciled at Billy's bedside before he passed, that did little for the long-term mental issues and sorrow etched on my little turtle. Grant tenderly sobbed in my arms after his dad's passing, "He only wanted me because he was dying." I stroked his hair and softly replied, "Dying was the way God made him wake up and see what was important to him. And that was you, Grantie. What a wonderful thing for him to learn."

One of the most endearing qualities about Grant, a.k.a. my little turtle, is that he loves me. He calls me Mama, and that breaks my heart and also makes me putty in his hands. I've said yes when I should have said no so many times. We now use the term codependent for this kind of counterproductive behavior. My photo is there in the dictionary next to the definition. I've learned that pleasing your children and guiding them are two opposite sets of behavior. All in all, Grant, my Civil War re-enactor since the age of five who had a small part in the movie *Gods and Generals*, has much to offer the world and me and his sister. He's just an old soul who perhaps took on these struggles with all the setbacks and strife as lessons for his quickest spiritual growth.

Like his father, women love Grant to a fault. He knows how to treat a woman or make promises to them; we aren't sure what his magic is. We only know it works again and again and again. Perhaps it's because Grant learned what all men yearn to know from listening to the still secrets that come from a female's soul. In a divorced home without a father, Dana and her girlfriends had the run of our house. Hours of taping themselves with their dance routines, eating bowls of macaroni and cheese, creating parties, pranking boys, sitting on the roof, planning their lives year after year, watching them grow. When summoned, I shared advice and stories about men, relationships, and love while Grant listened. Oh yes, he listened. God help the women in his world. Thanks for protecting Baby Grant, my turtle.

At that time of this writing, Grant is in his late twenties, with a rough road ahead of him. Sometimes it is the brightest who most clearly view the reality of life in the darkest and cruelest terms. Those who seek authentic reasons for being are often those who become most lost. All they see is senselessness as they watch what they describe as stupid people chasing nonsensical visions that lack substance. The phrase "ignorance is bliss" may be the reason people are statistically less happy today than they were in the '40s and '50s, in the age of post-materialism. We have gotten too smart and have missed the mark mistaking happiness as something you seek rather than something you already have in the simple bits of experiences that make up each day. If only he could see what I do in his eyes, he would have the courage to push through the night of growing pains and delusion into the morning. I have said these things and more, "Grantster, I know as sure as I'm talking with you that the sun always follows even the darkest night if we only persevere. All journeys are complex, filled with challenges, failures, and disappointments. It is also filled with warm summer nights, great books, and love. It's what we call life."

I loved that both Dana and Grant were with their Billy when he died at the young age of forty-six. Children never get over a divorce. They survive. They adapt. But it's harder for them. Both of my children fall into that category. As adults we rationalize our bad behaviors, saying that our kids are resilient and bounce back. On some level, they do, but it doesn't mean that they are immune to scars. Don't be so naive; no matter what the latest articles imply, divorce is a very big deal to everyone.

Billy and I had rocky moments, but all in all, our life was pretty typical of most marriages. I just didn't realize it. The final rock breaking up our home was my knowledge of his affair. Or maybe what truly broke us up was my lack of being able to more forward and get over it. I just couldn't allow my heart to forgive him. Pure ego took over and taped shut my ability to take some responsibility for what happened or didn't happen between us. There I was with Baby Dana in her white-and-pink one-piece lace jammies on the couch in front of the fireplace in the old house we made into our home. It was a cold winter night as we watched Care Bears, when I get this telephone call from a female voice.

"Is Billy there? We met in Philadelphia last month. He said he was interested in buying some horses."

I stopped. Frozen. My mind went blank. "What? We don't have enough property for horses!"

I huffed in confusion, holding a warm bottle in my other hand, not noticing it was dripping on the carpet. Then click. She hung up. It felt as though that click was a bomb that exploded right in the center of my living room, my life, my marriage, blowing my heart all over the room into a zillion little pieces. So I did what most girls do; I called my mom, which probably was not the best source of advice and comfort. She was a complex woman. In some areas, Queen Bee was wise beyond all comprehension. It was as if one part of her brain was gifted while the other part was warped and distorted in delusion.

Then Billy denied the entire thing until finally he was in the kitchen when she called. I'll never forget the ghostly white look on his face when I handed him the phone. He had nothing much to say except, "It was only once. I'm sorry. I was wrong." All of which were lies I learned some time afterward. After that, our life consisted of fights, regrets, and tears, and once again, my insistence of working this out. My pride bloomed into a giant wall of ivy as the tender lilies of my heart's love for him withered. I didn't realize until years later, upon reflection, of my inability to be rational and fair. We went to counseling and then redid our wedding vows, with our family members praying for healing, but I was praying for this fire inside me to go out.

After Grant was born, I became restless with that same fiery bitterness that started to corrupt my thoughts and disturb my peace of mind. I began to look outside my home, outside my marriage for something more. After Billy's affair, I turned to my safe haven: learning. My grandma gave me money for graduate school to keep me busy while I was a stay-at-home mom. Little did I know that a foreigner full of tales of lands and adventures across the world would pursue me for two years before I finally gave in. He was determined to befriend me as a professor at the Youngstown State University counseling department. I quite accidentally also got a part-time teaching position at Youngstown City Schools in adult basic education, which was at Choffin, where he worked as director of career education. He spoke so many languages and told me of the mountains in Greece, his white horse, and his love for the silliest parts of me. Even my daughter became enchanted when he spoke. Oh yes, he was always stopping over to chat. He wore me down. Then I gave him my heart and my soul! He never left his wife and eventually had to leave town for picking up a prostitute in the ghetto of Youngstown long after I had moved to Florida. His friends told me, "See what you did to him? He was Gattafied!" Oh Lord, why do I get blamed for every man's bad behavior.

I met this professor at Youngstown State University, the very same place where I met Billy. My ego still smarting from Billy's affair, this odd-looking, short, fat man with less than handsome looks spoke of love and poetry, creating beautiful images of things and places I never knew about. This was exotic to me as he uttered sweet nothings in other languages and told stories of growing up in Greece. This professor would call me from his office, munching on a piece of fruit, whispering, "Your ass is as succulent as the pear I'm nibbling on." Then he would call me from Greece when visiting his mother. He often delivered pear tortes to my mailbox for lunch early the next morning before school. He called me, his "little one with grape twigs toppling off her head as she falls from Mount Olympus." He made me feel alive and special. I was reborn as my marriage was stage-four terminal, fading into nothingness. I was living a double life. As any woman scorned, I had a bubbling antagonism fueling me to strike out and hurt and punish Billy for his indiscretions, playing the role of the homemaker and mother of two young children. This affair provided me a way of escape. It allowed me to avoid working on my "stuff." You know, the stuff we carry with us like luggage no matter how it drags us down, holds us back, and ruins our chance at getting the very thing we want most: to be loved. I was too frightened to let go of the emotional luggage that kept me from learning about myself. What would I find buried deep inside? Would I realize that I was responsible for what happened between Billy and myself and was a bad human being? I started thinking I was having a heart attack.

Then in the blink of an eye, the marriage died, leaving dirt and dead flowers in the yard as constant reminders of our failure in the dead of the winter. We had successfully managed to destroy our love, our history, and our family to the point of no return. Billy lost control against the power of my mother, who did everything she could to be the provider of our children's every whim and desire. It's hard to compete with the bank. He grew tired of warring with her and withdrew from all of it. I was not present in my own life, unwilling to see what my mom was doing and how Billy was recoiling from us. It was as though we bankrupted our love, withdrawing every warm feeling we had once felt without realizing it.

Then the worst happened. My cousin who kind of looks like me in a way—I'm not even going there—was a stylist who cut Billy's hair. Harmless, right? She did a lot more than style his hair, because I found out they were having an affair. At that point, no amount of forgiving deposits and commitment to our children could bring this love account back to the black. Billy quickly married my first cousin, which put the last nail on the coffin of ever reconciling. My psychologist told me once that Billy still loved me and wanted to avoid any chance of getting back together. I never asked Billy about that. But I think the psychologist may have been right. I should have asked Billy a lot of things. I let him get away with too much, and then I couldn't get him back. Women are the heart of the home, and that means keeping everyone connected.

When Billy was in his final days, my son, Grant, and I had one of the most memorable moments of my life. We had to wait for my cousin to leave, and we drove all the way across Alligator Alley so we could sneak into the hospital late one night and finally see Billy. We hid behind a big flower vase and watched in giggling silence until the coast was clear. Peering out of the sterile window, watching her drive away, we proceeded to find my ex.

Grant, a tall young man, entered first, standing like Peter Pan, and declared pleased as punch, "Dad, I brought you a surprise." Billy's hollow face, skinny and gaunt from the cancer that was eating away his life, looked up as I popped out from behind like a bunny. I didn't know what to expect or how Billy would handle this little surprise. I stared, half afraid and half excited after so many years of absolutely no contact. There was this man whom I had loved, sick and weak, breaking me in two. Crocodile tears poured down his cheeks, and he said softly, "What took you so long?" I moved in to embrace him. "You are still so pretty." He continued in tears, "You kiss me like Dana does." It was at that moment that all my anger washed away and all I felt was love. He went on, "I did so many bad things to you. Things you wouldn't imagine."

I put my finger every so tenderly on his lips, "I don't care. I love you, and I always will." The war was over, and we again joined the same side, united, hand in hand, heart to heart.

It was in that split second that I turned and gazed at my baby boy, Grant Charles Kirkwood. In his eyes, I felt all the moments he missed having two parents in the same room at the same time. For the first time, Grant watched, grinning as we both tried to advise him on matters about life. Matters that we should have addressed long ago. He grinned as we gave him a hard time. He welcomed our disciplinary warnings as though they were Christmas gifts.

Then we shared the latest news about our daughter, who was then a senior at Miami University in the Gables. Dana's best friend from Liberty, Lindsay, was getting married back home the following week. Billy asked if he could come. Looking a bit bewildered, I said, "Of course, you can come with us wherever we go." We kissed and left, not knowing at the time that I would never speak with him again.

My cousin had given orders to hospital staff in attempts to keep me from seeing him, but she did allow our kids to see him at least one more time before he died. Billy's mother was also in town and called to let us know that Billy was near the end. She had anointed his feet, and everyone was there. Dana drove in from Miami during her finals. Grant and I drove in from Coral Springs. The night he passed, I sat alone waiting while my children were upstairs in the hospital room with their dying dad. At this point, the only things that mattered to me were my kids and helping Billy transition as peacefully as possible. His mother came down and mentioned, "Billy asked to see you again." I told Grant. I wish I had been more aware of how little time he had left. I would have taken a day off. I should have taken the day off. I wish I would have taken the day. It had been a long, painful bout of cancer. Dana and Grant bid farewell to their dad on April 19, 2006. As soon as we were on the highway, we saw fires on both sides of the road, in the fields. An intuitive told me that Billy would pass and she saw fire. This was it.

I first lost my grandma on Thanksgiving morning. I lost the father of my children a few months later. There was a fire in my belly. One less person to lean on through my struggles, which were about to fuel higher. Since I was not welcome at the funeral in Naples, Florida, there was a beautiful service with a picnic following in New Castle, Pennsylvania, honoring my children and recognizing my presence in Billy's life, hosted by his surviving mother, brother, and sister. My mother collapsed at his memorial; little did I know in less than a year, she would be gone as well. Everyone came from far and near, and it was one of the kindest gestures his family ever gave me. I felt grateful and honored.

Funny thing about death, you may know it's coming, but you are never prepared, and it's so damn permanent. It's actually still difficult for me to wrap my head around. Maybe it's because real death doesn't exist. I know I feel Billy around me more now than I ever have. In the secret place of my soul, I know our love was still very much alive, and I feel his presence often.

Yes, Billy was the marriage of my life. In retrospect, I can see three problems that made the odds of our marriage lasting unlikely, and some were not actually our fault. Billy and I were too young. Neither one of us knew what we were doing or the seriousness of a marital commitment. I've learned that the two most important questions anyone will ask themselves about their future are these: Where am I going (career), and whom am I taking with me (partner, lifestyle)?

Second, my mother was intrusive and jealous beyond comprehension. She did everything she could to deteriorate our relationship. His family wasn't too much better, except they took a different approach. They were evangelical Christians. Not sure you can convey how they acted and put Christian in the same sentence.

The affairs didn't help. Some women can get past them. Some can't. I couldn't get over the thoughts of his jeans on the floor next to someone else's. The little sweet nothings he says to me, I plagued myself wondering if he said them to others. I used to joke and say it would be easier if he had died. That wasn't true. That was and still is agonizing. I just can't believe he's gone. And I want to definitively know one thing: Where is everyone rushing off to? I love it here. I have a few things to discuss with the maker, like pestilence, illness, and the hardship of animals, but it's a beautiful planet.

Years later, long after Billy and I divorced, living in South Florida, I met a sassy, nonchalant friend. Debbie. She had long, dark, curly hair and self-confident style. Anyone could tell she was a born-and-bred New Yorker. Add to that being Italian and firstborn. She was so much more street-smart than me. She would always ask me, "Why do you smile at everyone?" She had a straightforward manner, working in the brokerage world of mostly men, and possessed the female wisdom most of us only wish we had. She saw it all. The men cheating, the women in power, and the energy that was mandatory to stay in such a fast-paced world. She gave me a phrase that later became our theme for all the stories of headaches and heartaches. I think women over forty, at least, will understand. Our mantra is "What did you expect?"

When a guy cheats on his wife, cheats with his secretary, and now cheats on you, what did you expect?

Debbie and I now laugh about that because we have been hurt so many times.

You have to laugh. That's certainly better than throwing yourself into the local body of water, waiting for an alligator to gobble you up. A good friend is worth the thousands it would cost for a shrink. She makes me laugh; not many men can make that claim.

Think about it. He married you after he had an affair with you. So why do you think that he would not cheat on you?

What did you expect?

I think women expect men to be different with them. I think women are more evolved spiritually than men. I think women are more honest. I also think that when a woman decides to cheat, she is aware of the consequences beforehand. We've thought long and hard before picking up that key to the hotel room, meeting him for drinks, sneaking off for a quickie at lunch.

I don't think men think much at all, especially in the area of relationships. I'm not male-bashing here. I know a great number of men with high intelligence who lack a deep sense of morality and just kind of land wherever they are in love due, in part, to habit. Our little guys are so simple; they just want to know where to park their car, get their beer, and keep their toothbrush. Throw in some great food and sex, and they are settled and content.

It could be that men are inborn hunters and are programmed deep within their DNA to win at any cost. In doing so, they have grown to have thick skin, wipe their tears, and move on in spite of their losses. They are bred to slay the enemy without looking back on the way to victory. But when it comes to sex, men are driven by thoughts that emanate from below the waist, or what I like to call the kitchen sink, and that is where woman rule the kingdom.

CHAPTER 7

I've Got You Under My Skin

He was a part of me. I've lost track of how many times I went back to him. I was on the road with him from 1975 to 1981, again in 1995, and then on and off again until 2008. Whenever love's light went out, my hopes for a normal married life vanished, and I was lost without a compass, I ran back to him. It seems pathetic now as I see it in print. But in some twisted way, I thought each time that if he saw me in a different light, he might realize I was the one.

If I had been as committed to my career as I was to Frankie, I would be running my own private Ivy League school by now or working as a psychiatrist doing research. Talk about determination. Call it imprinting gone wild or the typical father issue, but I surely wasn't going to let this go, in part because of that old Pentecostal brainwashing resonating in my head: "You only sleep with someone you marry." I'd already bedded him, or maybe it was that he bedded me. Either way, I gave him the power to have a hypnotic hold on me. I wanted him forever, with a fairytale ending, so sleeping with him was my way of giving my heart to him.

I think I really went for me. It was my choice. Frankie didn't lure me. I could have not gone. At least I was never involved with him while I was married. I subconsciously knew there were others. I must have. After all, I'm not a moron earning two master's degrees in counseling. Like many of my clients, I deluded myself, thinking I was different. I wasn't. I began to see that he wasn't who I had imagined. Maybe this was my way of forcing myself to see it through and gain insight, or maybe I'm full of shit. I tried to look at him without my inner child screaming, "I love you, I love you, I love you." I'm not sure what the lure was for him. I never asked. I think I was afraid to hear the worst. I was nothing to him. I'd like to say it no longer matters, but it does. I can't lie anymore. I can't be tough and strong all the time. I am coming out to my broken self and hoping the little girl inside can join me and heal.

Truthfully, isn't there always another side hidden deep inside each of us? I sometimes walk through the mall, looking at people, wondering what their inner child must look like and what fairy tales still live with them in each breathing moment. We are bred to be the strongest of our litter, survive the odds, thrive, and hide the weakest parts of ourselves. In today's society, it means not just fitting in, but creating the best in ourselves to gain the admiration and acceptance of others. Whether it's marrying well to be a pillar of the community or becoming a self-made millionaire to have the power to create, it all comes down to how others see us as a success or a failure.

I was still living the glamorous life as a single but devoted lady to a man I didn't even see. I didn't have to cook, clean, wash his clothes, or give two hoots about what he truly thought. I only had this romantic vision of life with him that kept those steamy phone calls coming in, and we were all pretty content. At least, I was. My daughter had a little flat two streets over from Ocean Drive in South Beach, and if I wanted to break free, I went there to shop, lie on the beach, and share some umbrella fruity alcohol beverage with my true soul mate, Dana Nicole Kirkwood.

I even started doing community theatre and had a lead in a play in Stuart, Florida, at the Barn Theatre. There's so much New York and New Jersey talent here that community work is much more professional than most Midwestern towns where I grew up. I was terrible at acting, much like Marilyn in some of her first roles, but it worked for the part I played, and even my teacup Yorkie had a part. She stole the show, jumping out of my purse right on cue and sat on the couch as I continued my lines. Her presence helped me become more natural. I think the hardest job in the world is to be an actor. Each of us struggle to find our authentic selves at each stage in our lives, then a part comes and actors are asked to forget it all and jump into the skin of someone else. Bravo! I have such respect for those who can manage to keep their sanity through it all. I have a difficult time just figuring out who April is and where my soul and my personality collide.

So it is my ultimate Frankie Valli substitute, number three, who has been by far the most painful and exhausting in love thus far. There is a rule of sorts in astrology that says if you don't learn your lessons during the first half of your life, they are presented more harshly and severely during the second half. Shit.

I sat there half wondering during our entire conversation, How did I miss him all these years? I just couldn't believe that we hadn't crossed paths before, because it seemed that we ran in the same social circles in a small town. The night I met Ronnie, the lyrics from Frankie's song "My Eyes Adored You" bounced around in my head while my heart fluttered with every inhale and exhale he took. He's one of those soft-spoken guys who draw you in more by what he doesn't say. You know, the puppy you find on the corner, whimpering and following you to your car. His boyish charms make you want to save him from his childish need to be protected and cared for. He's the guy they are talking about when pop psych books describe men who are enmeshed with their moms and hate women for needing them. It's the "I hate you, don't leave me" scenario played out over and over with various women throughout his life. His employees at his music store called them "Ron's rentals." WTF. Little did I know that it was me who would need protecting. Be forewarned, there are guys like him under every rock.

Ron is the man who made me wake up from the dream of what life would have been like with Mr. Valli. He and I must have been always six degrees near one another. He was the man of the town. He was the celebrity of Youngstown in the '70s, '80s, and '90s. I'll never forget Frankie warning me, "You'll become his wife, and you'll be miserable as he continues to cheat with another April or perhaps many Aprils. Get yourself some nice doctor who is respected. You can't win, April." Oh, but I can. I'm with you, I thought to myself. As I write this, I keep picturing myself seeing him again and discussing this little story of mine. I rehearse it over and over and over in my mind as I walk, eat, type, and breathe. I imagine myself dropping over dead like one of those goats that faint when something startles them. He startles me, brings me to life, takes all the air in the room. Shit, I better not see him, or I may just drop over.

I thought, Ron is the only guy who could replace Frankie in my life. We met right after his mom passed.

Ron's wavy, long, coiffed black hair; his expensive veneers; and his gigantic black eyes made me weak. I resisted the urge to reach across the table and run my fingers through that hair as his eyes flashed a glance into mine. Remember what I said about putting out on the first date? I forced myself to keep my hands to myself and my legs closed that night. Besides, he said he had to rush to Pittsburgh to pick up his dad at the airport. His dad had never flown in a plane, of course; I found out that about ten years too late.

I know this may sound shallow, but I was impressed with his rugged, worn leather jacket and black BMW. Ronnie played the role of the antiestablishment, rocking-roller type with cash. He controlled the town and knew he had no need to put on airs. He would walk into a bank, sit among the corporate types all in suits, and get a loan for $100,000, wearing tennis shoes and a T-shirt. That is so cool, I thought. My rebellious side loved his disregard for convention. I could tell things were important to this man. And I liked that because the nicer things in life were, and still are, important to me. Little did I realize that I was a thing. Being in South Beach during a snowstorm in Ohio is fabulous, and that's a fact. Money doesn't make you happy, but it makes being miserable bearable.

Another selling point for me was the fact Ron is 100 percent from-the-old-country Italian. All I can say is amore! Although not all of them know how to treat a woman, they do know how to make a woman feel good. I don't mean that in a purely sexual context, although I haven't known any of them to disappoint between the sheets, or on the couch, or in the backseat of a car.

Like Frankie and Billy, Ron was in the music business. It started as a little pawnshop in the good old Mafia days in downtown Youngstown. He and his family worked hard and eventually rented instruments to area schools and did sound for all the clubs from Pittsburgh to Cleveland. He didn't play an instrument but has grown his business to a multi-million-dollar business in less than ten years. He always said, "I make dreams happen." Sweet dreams or nightmares, I'm not quite sure, but he definitely makes it happen.

However, what's the very, very best thing about Ron?

He looks like Frankie Valli. It's like the cliché: you could have knocked me over with a feather. That's how you could describe my feelings that first night with Ron. I kept thinking to myself, I hit the mother lode. Bingo! I found the golden egg. I won the lottery! You get the idea.

I drove back to my old farmhouse that night, with my heart soaring again for the first time in many years. I had finally found my man, or at least the best substitute for Frankie Valli I could have ever conjured up. Cruising along, singing to the Commodores, I realized that I didn't catch Ron's last name. I pondered for a moment of common sense and then turned up the volume on the radio even louder and threw caution to the wind. I was in love. Again, at the age of forty-one, and hopefully for the last time. My heart soared back through the clouds into the stratosphere. I was going to marry a successful Italian and be an Italian wife and make sauce on Sundays for all our kids and plant tomatoes in the backyard.

You see, I was ready for love again. It had been about six years since Billy and I divorced. I went back to Frankie for a brief time, but it was obvious—painfully obvious to me and my heart—that we shouldn't be together. I was a woman who had chased her man for more than two decades at that point, and the awareness that being Frankie Valli's woman was not going to happen became, in part, my decision. I never went to see him alone; that way, I would never get too close to being hurt again.

Yes, we can hunt for answers in the wrong places. Knowing what I know about love and myself, I can say that is exactly what I did with Frankie. The soul needs to find a connection with others. Love is the source of our vitality, recharging those who dare to drink the elixir to find new hope and renewed energy. We're devoted to finding love. And we have plenty of help in our quest. There is a plethora of books, blogs, magazine articles, and movies about our quest for love. Have you ever scanned the headlines on magazine covers near the checkout line at a grocery or drug store? Who hasn't? I challenge you to count the number of headlines that scream something like "How to land your man in a month! But we often pick the wrong man and wonder why it didn't work out.

When I moved in with Ron in the summer of 2009, I got caught up in what it would be like to live with Frankie Valli. That's where my mind and heart were at the time. It didn't seem to bother Ronnie that I thought he looked very much like Frankie Valli. The deep, dark eyes that sparkled when he smiled. The wide grin that dazzled people, particularly women. The silky smooth voice. The "I'm in charge" attitude.

Those two could be twin souls. I'm still dealing with the emotional pain of realizing that Frankie and Ron are just who they are. Two Italians from the old school, uneducated, narcissistic, and most interested in themselves and their needs over anyone else's. It may be a car, real estate, a wife, or forgiveness. Whatever the case, when they present themselves as giving human beings, it is most certainly underlined with a need to control and be seen as the great guy they aren't.

I think back to one of my last intimate conversations with Frankie. We were in New Castle, Pennsylvania, lying on the bed, just bullshitting about life, and I watched him as always put his french fries on top of the meat on his burger then squash it all together with the bun. I told him about Ron and that he was married and shared the dirty details. All of the promises to begin a life together that never actualized. I loved lying on the bed, no shoes, just he and I alone, talking. Once again, I sought out his advice more like a dad than a lover. Frankie kindly said to me, "April, if he's seeing you, he probably has other girlfriends too. Believe me, you aren't the only one. And if by some slim chance he does leave his wife, you will become the wife and someone will replace you." Well, is that calling the kettle black or what!

Nothing sexual happened between me and Frankie then. We walked together as always, with his arm wrapped around my shoulders, his hand cupping me closer to him. That was one of the most romantic embraces in my life. He always walked with me like that, so comforting and nurturing.

A couple I met through Frankie was also at the concert that night. They had spent the day shopping with him. The wife came up to me after seeing our interaction and asked, "What did you two do in the room?" Odd question, I know, and truly none of her business.

As always, naive me sweetly responded, "Nothing. We just talked."

The husband jumped in. "We haven't seen him this happy in a long time."

I smiled. It was a wonderful feeling to think I could finally make the man feel good.

But not all the times Frankie and I met were like warm, mushy reunions. In Pittsburgh, I took Ron backstage to meet Frankie. Holy shit. What happened next came as a total shock to me. I was totally blown away when his longtime road manager ran like a thief in the night while Frankie followed, strutting like a puffed-up peacock, pointing his finger in my face, screaming at me. I was shocked and had no idea what had happened. I stood there, shrinking back to seven years of age. I actually felt small. I had read an article in the *National Enquirer* about an airline stewardess selling her story about her affair with Frankie. I don't know how I do these things, but I found his e-mail address somehow. There is definitely some weird karma going on between us. I wrote to Frankie, sharing how awful it was that she would sell intimate details of their love life. I guess Toni, his wife, read the e-mail, and the rest is a total train wreck. His finger was waving manically like a flag in my face while his voice hit falsetto pitches I hadn't heard for years. Worst of all, Ron stood in the background, dazed and confused. To say the least, that meeting didn't go too smoothly. Ron still gives me shit about that one. I felt absolutely terrible. I didn't know it was a family e-mail. Who does that!

There's something very revealing about returning to where you grew up. One warm fall day when the leaves were just starting to transform into their brilliant reds, golds, and browns, I walked from my mom's to my grandma's white house where I grew up. With the gravel under my feet, I reminisced, mentally seeing my kids running to the screen door, trying to avoid the wrath of the swans who lived in my uncle Billy's pond in the back. If reality is all happening in the mind, I was again filled with joy when others would only see an old, broken-down house now silent and still, in need of a total makeover. I sauntered past the white fence, beyond the maple tree that was planted when I was born, to the creek where I used to catch crawfish as a little girl. I suddenly fell to my knees, tears flowing down my face. I was looking for something, anything that was once from my family's life. An old fork, a shovel, a pan, anything that could prove it all really happened. Items I once considered trash now seemed to be more valuable than any piece of jewelry I ever owned. Everything was rusty and deteriorated. I looked everywhere, my hands shifting in the dirt. I picked up a stone, kissed it, and put it in my pocket like it was the answer to what had gone so wrong. And so I began my search back at the beginning of the story. I remembered hoping to fact-check reality versus fantasy to acquire at least some understanding.

My quest began at Stambaugh Auditorium, where I attended church and Junior League meetings. I quietly entered and respectfully asked if I could go in and sit. A little old man dressed in a navy night-guard uniform smiled. "I don't see why not, miss." I walked down the aisles I had so many times before and took a seat on the velvet chairs. The stage was dark. Songs echoed through my being, with faces that went with feelings I had long forgotten. I don't think I moved for two hours. I remember standing and looking way up on the balcony to the light where the projector came through. I saw a figure but couldn't make out who it was. I walked up the marble steps, around the corner, up some more, and stepped ever so carefully in dark. It seemed to take forever. There Frankie was, sitting with a brown sweater on, his elbow resting on the seat, saying in a monotone manner, neither angry nor happy, "I've been waiting for you." The night guard tapped me on the shoulder, and I almost jumped out of my skin. Was it a dream? Some kind of message? I walked out more confused than before I entered.

Driving back to my mom's house, now in need of repair, I continued this spiritual journey to when I was six years old, traveling four hours on a hot summer day to Cedar Point in Sandusky, Ohio. Before Disney World became the king of amusement parks, Cedar Point was one of the best in the country. But we didn't go to Cedar Point for the rides. I wanted to see my man, Mr. Frankie Valli. Even at a prepubescent age, I was entranced, secretly wishing my name was Sherry. My mom made me a pageant banner that spelled out "Frankie" in sparkles with a matching straw hat that had a glitter "Frankie" on it too. I was so worried we would be late. Being only as big as a peanut—my aunt still calls me that—I could nuzzle up close to the bandstand, pushing through the teenagers. During one of the songs, his saw me and pointed to me. Me! My family stood a foot or two back and watched carefully. Then the magic happened. Frankie brought me onstage. I was speechless. Frankie has made me pretty much speechless since then too.

After the show, I got to go backstage, where he gave me some pumpkin seeds. I wouldn't eat them. Are you kidding me? He touched them. "I'm not eating those ever," I said handing them to Grandma to hold. Not because of germs or anything like that. I wanted them as a souvenir. Grandma and I put them in a scrapbook, proudly looking at my gift. I had pumpkin seeds from Frankie Valli. Who else could say that? In my little mind, no one. Just me. And that made me special.

In the '60s, before computers, cable, or cell phones, it was a real task just to find out when and where stars were performing. I would have to go to the bookstore and look at newspapers in nearby towns, scan magazines, and wait for some glimmer of hope that soon the Four Seasons would pass through my vicinity. I was a relentless little girl. I may have been tiny at the time, but my energy and determination were huge.

Each summer I went to the Four Seasons concerts. It was kind of like an unspoken understanding with my family and girlfriends. I began to feel a kinship to this man, as though we shared the same history. He was family to me. I was his little girl on the road. I never once let it enter my mind that I would be more. I mean, what could be better than being his daughter. You can divorce your wife, I thought to myself, but you can never divorce your children.

As you can well imagine, after we had been intimate in Youngstown, Ohio, the entire vibe changed dramatically for me. I traveled to Syracuse, New York; Flint, Michigan; Cleveland, Ohio; and every spot in between. Frankie was in his prime and fiercely sexual. I had decided my role in his life was going to a whole new level. "Who loves you, pretty baby," I sang to myself as I danced in the suite when he wasn't around. I was grooming myself to be his wife. Everything I did had that end goal in mind: college, exercise, clothing, work ethic and being hip, aware, and well bred. I only needed to grow up a little more.

For a brief moment in my existence, I got to live it too. I enjoyed waiting backstage like a queen waiting for her king to finish his duties. I dressed in the best Saks Fifth Avenue could offer and elegantly acted the part. I graciously worked the room, acknowledging those around Frankie and his band. I learned the protocol of being a star's significant other. I also grew to understand that men love being waited on and treated with respect by someone who is appreciative for his presence in her life.

After the shows, when the press and the guests had gone, we'd bid good night to everyone and head off for some private time. I felt on top the world. You know that feeling. You're on your man's arm or holding hands, and every eye in the room is on you when you leave. Very few things in this world give a woman that kind of feeling.

In the mornings after, the air felt like a dense fog had descended. We would come down into the restaurant for breakfast, and all eyes were upon us. I looked awkwardly down, pretending to be oblivious to my surroundings. His buds wore a knowing grin slapped on their faces. Frankie got a few thumbs-up with cheesy innuendoes as though I were deaf. One of the most unkind gestures he made was when he introduced me to his comedian buddy. He said, "This is Virginia, and I have my sharpshooter." Yuck.

But that wasn't the most heartrending of memories of me and Frankie. A few were more like an avalanche tumbling and crushing my world, not leaving as much as a trace that I even existed to Frankie. It always began with Frankie's silence. He was disappearing, distancing himself from me both physically and emotionally. Then there were occasions that he made phone calls, whispered, and abruptly woke me up to the fact that this tryst was not going to last. Every damn time, no matter how perfect I tried to be, when he was ready, he sent me home. No questions asked. I was to leave politely, like a lady, if I ever hoped to be invited back again.

"OK," I softly replied, thinking, But next time you won't send me home. You'll keep me. You'll see.

It was I, not Frankie, who had to open my eyes no matter how bright and painful the sun was, burning a hole in my being. This was a lose-lose for me. After the incident with Billy in Chicago, I don't think I could have done anything to win back Frankie's image of me. When my kids were old enough, I took them to the Four Seasons concerts with me. My stomach rolled when I first introduced them. I wasn't sure how he would react. Would he ignore us? Not have time for us? On the contrary, Frankie welcomed the kids into his presence and the pressroom, making them feel comfortable right away. He was so charming when he wanted to be.

"Do you know I have known your mom since she was this big," he said, raising his hand to about three feet off the floor.

We chatted, and my stomach calmed. Then he asked, "But can your mom cook?"

Dana and Grant looked at each other blankly and then back at me, finally returning their gaze to him. Dana blurted out, "She makes great homemade sauce."

I exhaled. I could have fallen over from lack of air. Thank goodness. Dana brings it again, I thought, smiling at my two adorable kids. I've always been able to count on Dana to defend me and uplift me. She did it again!

I admit I had ulterior motives for taking Dana and Grant with me. First, I wanted my two darlings to meet Frankie, who was behind the songs they memorized due to my listening to those same hits over and over and over again. Second, and more honestly, Dana and Grant kept me from letting his voice, his breath, his air, melt every ounce of common sense I ever thought I had. I couldn't let myself be that easy. I couldn't fall back into his bed, giving in to this hypnotic power that gave Frankie the ability to summon me at will. How close is too close to be tempted? It doesn't take much for me when I make someone a demigod. Just a simple hello makes me weak and helpless.

I last saw Mr. Valli at the Hard Rock in Hollywood, Florida, in 2008 after the death of my mom. I had taken a racy photo of myself in a Jersey Boys T-shirt from the Broadway hit show and sent it backstage for him. A few minutes before the lights dimmed, a security man came up and said he would be more than happy to escort us backstage after the show. My aunt Ginny, uncle Chuck, and daughter, Dana, were with me. I was so excited and so frightened. My mind was spinning like I had just gulped down a glass of champagne: What in the hell am I doing? I sent this semi-pornographic photo to Frankie? How ridiculous. Why am I even here? Oh God, here I am making the same mistakes again. I'm chasing him.

In a few seconds, the lights dimmed, and he entered the stage with the same charisma and talent as years before. The songs flooded my heart with contradictory feelings of intoxication and aversion for this megastar, simultaneously turning my brain to mush. For an instant, I seemed to have jumped out of my own way and saw the truth: this guy made me a total freaking train wreck.

After the show, we waited in the greenroom for Mr. Valli to grace us with his presence. Seriously? I looked around the room, and what I saw repulsed me. It was as though someone gave me a glimpse of what I could become. Scattered among the room were fifty-plus South Florida women who were over-tanned, wearing tight jeans and accentuating their fake boobs and injected lips. They all had long, straw-looking, over-bleached hair, and I wondered just how many of these once-hot girls bedded the one and only Napoleonic legend. I felt cheap and dirty and disgusted; that was until he came into the room.

I became jelly ready to leap into his arms and let him whisk me off to his world. Thank goodness, after a moment of insanity, I regained consciousness and got just plain annoyed. Tonight he acted weird though. He didn't move around, making his stops, welcoming guests as usual. (I later found out that he had the flu.) KC and the Sunshine Band was waiting to chat with Frankie as well. I became even more incensed at their fake demeanor—until Frankie glanced my way and motioned for me to come closer. I smiled warmly like a first-grader who just got her very first Valentine. OK, this is it. I've got to get my game on. We embraced, and I playfully asked, winking and flirting, "May I have that photo back? You just never know where it could land." He laughed with that slightly devious aura of his and sent someone to get the photo.

Suddenly someone brought him the phone, and he disappeared from the moment into his own personal space. I saw it pointedly clear. The ghosts of the past had not been exorcised and were still hanging in the shadows. The pain flashed before my eyes. I mustered up every thought of every bit of therapy and common sense that I could to block out my heart's imprint. When he returned, I moved like a robot ever so closely and whispered what I had wanted to say to him for years but was too afraid, "I'm never coming to see you again. You never loved me. You never cared, and I have loved you since I was a little girl. Maybe in another life you will see what you had in me."

Now every Frankie Valli fan knows he has had hearing loss. In fact, I dated one of his doctor's sons. Life is strange, isn't it! So adding that to rumors he had the flu, I'm not sure if he heard me. This is a question that still haunts me now and then. When I listen to the radio, look through photo albums, glance across the dinner table at Ron, I wonder what in the hell was going through his head when I said goodbye for the last time. These are the kinds of silly, useless details girls relive over and over and finally put away until the next heartbreak gives us reason to shut down and crush the name of love. Frankie just stared at me and watched me turn my back and return to my true family.

At times, I think I'm still wandering in the deep darkness of my soul, unable or unwilling to leave that painful comfort zone where my heart resided for my entire life. You know, that place that at one time served you and protected you but is now only a flawed belief system that hinders your growth. Still, you resist, letting go in spite of the damage it's doing. After years of people saying "What was she thinking?" I have begun to ask myself that same question.

Sometimes I'm embarrassed that I am the only one who must look in the mirror and say, "You, Miss April, are not Cinderella. Find your own damn slipper and buy your own castle."

Have I said goodbye to Frankie? It's a very long goodbye, and I find that the physical farewell occurs well before the emotional one. In truth, Frankie is still very much under my skin, and unless I cut up my body, he is a part of who I am today. What hurts most is that he never even truly said hello. What I mean by that is that Frankie doesn't know me and quite obviously couldn't care less. He never stopped long enough to look beyond the mascara and manicured toes to see that just possibly, I could be someone who might just offer him more than a one-night stand. He'll never do it now after this book, and perhaps nothing was going to change this fact even if I slipped away with my hands in my lap, my legs crossed, and my lips shut.

CHAPTER 8

Let's Hang On

When it became apparent—again—that I would not be the next Mrs. Frankie Valli (this is starting to sound a lot like the movie *Groundhog Day*), I gave up on men for a while. I stenciled little gold stars on my living room ceiling at my grandma's house where I moved in with the kids after my thirteen-year marriage ended in divorce. It must have taken me over six months to complete. They used to tell us in counseling classes that it normally takes approximately one month of mourning for every year we were in the relationship. Oh God, I'm in big trouble. I'm going to need to get more walls to paint. Dana and Grant needed my attention, so I dove headlong into being a single mom. My kids became my focus by which I measured my worth as a human being. As a guidance counselor, I was only too familiar with the conflicts of blended families. It can be a disaster with Mom being both a disciplinarian and comfort keeper.

I do believe that the man is the head of the home and the woman is the heart of the home. Both roles are equally important. Who is to model what is right for children if not the parents? Is it the school's sole responsibility to model morals and character development? Absolutely not. As a social worker employed in an inpatient mental health facility for adolescents and teens, I was amazed at the number of parents who refused to take responsibility for the mess in their homes. They wanted to write the check and have us fix them. Of course, that's impossible without the foundation changing. And we wonder why kids are in and out of institutions and why there's a rise in addictions and increase in mortality rates of our youth, our future, our America. Kids learn by what we do, not by what we say.

If you wind up as a single mom, all I can say is God bless you. It's exhausting to be all things to everyone all the time, and you aren't going to be perfect. It's tiring, yes, but it must be done for the betterment of the children. When my grandpa was going into surgery shortly before he passed, he said only this, "Take care of the little ones." Running around, trying to find the next guy, who is in most cases the wrong guy, doesn't help the children.

It is for those very strong beliefs in family, which are growing more and more with each goodbye to loved ones passing on, that I'm glad I stayed in Youngstown near family. Despite my love of the glitzy lifestyle, I'm still a Midwestern girl at heart, with a strong work ethic. I guess you can take the girl out of the Midwest, but you can't take the Midwest out of the girl. I know, I know. Some of you city folks may think that's crazy, but it's true. Those who have lived in a small town for any length of time, particularly in the Midwest, know what I'm talking about. We're certainly a different type of person than those from other parts of the United States.

I felt it was best to remain "home" with them. No matter where I live, Youngstown will always be home, whether the world views homegrown Youngstown Congressman Traficant as a saint or a Mafia-linked mobster. I grew up there, my mother grew up there, and so did my cousins, my aunts, and my uncles, so I thought it would be best for Dana and Grant to be raised there as well. We settled into a daily routine of the kids going to school and me heading off to work.

One day, not long after 9/11, I was online, shopping at Nordstrom, when I received an instant message from someone I didn't know. I nonchalantly glanced at the picture on the messenger and thought, Not bad. Nice smile actually. I replied back, and we started up a conversation. I wasn't sure where this was leading, but I stopped visualizing myself in designer clothes I couldn't afford and started chatting with someone online. What a novel idea! How weird to meet someone on a computer. I waited for his words to appear on the screen.

He said that he was Italian—no surprise—and that he loved music and was in the industry. The more he wrote, the more he turned the door handle, touching all my weak spots even after I had closed my heart a few years prior. The idea of love was like a shot in the arm to my entire being. This guy, Ron, also loved animals. That did it. My interest was piqued. I loved animals. I was raised back in the woods, with few neighbors, and animals were my playmates when Aunt Ginny and Aunt Rosie went away. Any man who loves animals gets an A-plus in my heart.

It was that simple instant message that turned my world upside down. I was instantly awoken from a trance by this stranger. This should have been a red flag for imprinters like me. Life is queer at times, or perfectly timed, depending upon how the stars are aligned. We had been dating for a few weeks, and Ron had met the kids and come to our little farmhouse to pick me up like an actual date. He had told me he was separated and living at his store, so using his cell number was always the best way to reach him. He was full of shit, I realize that now. Back then, it never occurred to me to call the court-house for records or do any sort of research; it just would have seemed dishonest.

This particular day was more of a nightmare for Ron and a walk-up call for my soul. Dana, an innocent teenager, joyfully blurted out to her language arts class while they were chatting about a poem, "I'm so happy. My mom just met this awesome guy who owns Legend Music. My mom loves him." The tall blond instructor stopped dead in her tracks. It turns out that Dana's language arts teacher was the sister of Ron's wife, and the dirty laundry was hanging in that classroom for all to see. Well, guess who found out before the first bell rang.

I don't blame Ron's wife, but I heard that all hell broke loose. Ron told his wife this kid was crazy. Why is it that every man I know says we are "crazy" when he gets busted? Really! She didn't believe him, as this was only one of many simi-lar scenarios for this mother of three. Still, she wanted proof, so she called me and said, "Hello, I'm calling on behalf of our sales staff at AT&T about your cell phone connection to others. The last call you made was **********. Is that correct?" Like a dummy, I chatted with her. That act alone was proof to anyone with a brain that I a new girl to the world of affairs. Rule one: never speak to wife of lover.

An hour later she phoned me as herself. That conversa-tion was more direct. "I'm Mrs. *******. Are you seeing my husband?" I wanted to choke on my spit. Not long ago I was in this very position, asking the questions to Billy's girlfriend.

Like a moron, I said, "Oh no, I'm so sorry. I fell in love with him at first sight. I think he loves me too."

The wife snapped back as if gasping for air, "I'm staying here for the sake of my family. I'll call you back." I never heard from her after that.

Dana felt guilty. Grant was disappointed again. I was crushed. I started to stencil my dining room in a summer garden theme this time. The diversion didn't stop the hurt. I was beyond disappointed. I was broken.

I should have changed my cell, blocked his calls, forgotten we ever crossed paths. There was one slight issue: he had my heart. I would do anything for him, and that included being reduced to having a tawdry, ugly affair for one more look into his eyes. How did I consciously manage to convince myself this heinous behavior was acceptable? Well, at the time I was delving into the studies of the Kabbalah where they often permit a man to have several female companions. It's odd, we often use scriptures to our own devices to rationalize what we know is wrong.

After several nights of tears, Ron promised me he would file for divorce right after Christmas. I could understand waiting until the holidays were over; I mean, I'm a team player and wanted this to be as easy for everyone as possible. So I sat and began the waiting game. A game that took perseverance and practice to stay focused on my goal: getting my Frankie Valli copy. I was over the top, losing all sense of integrity. I'd make love in any backseat of any car, any crappy hotel, anywhere, anytime. By the way, if he's tight with his money at the beginning of the heat of passion, just wait, it's not going to get better. We never recognize those cues when our panties are down at our ankles. I even reduced myself to frequenting a dirty Days Inn, not even a Hilton. See, in my mind, once I had crossed the line and became intimately connected to him, I was finished, putty to be played with, no longer owning my body or my mind. I no longer had a brain or a rational thought left. That's why I've only slept with seven men in my entire life. Giving myself to seven other human beings is an immensely large amount of energy to give away to the wrong people.

He had three kids. I never intentionally wanted to hurt anyone. Now I see I hurt everyone. Christmas came and went as I sat waiting for my life to begin, and we finally rang in the new year after four long months. Then my world crashed. He might as well have put a knife in my heart—the slow bleed had begun. Ron said his brother forbade him to leave, because it would ruin their business partnership. (What is he, seven? Since when do you ask your brother permission to live your life?) His father said Ron was so in love with me that he threatened to throw himself into the Mahoning River. (I don't think you can drown in there, by the way.) I raged on and on, mascara running, choking on my spit, heaving in heartache, until he kissed me. Then he promised to leave after tax season. I don't have enough fingers and toes to count how many times he gave me exact dates after that. Each lie took a little piece of the love I had for him and burned it to cinders and smoke. I know now this is a common lie men tell their mistresses. I hate to use that word to describe myself. But I was just that— a mistress waiting for my man to leave his wife for me. He had given me every excuse in the book, and I wanted to believe him in spite of every living person I knew trying to get me to dump his rotten ass. I began to cover for him, making excuses, lying in bed alone on holidays, hoping that he would wake up and smell the coffee. I was the baby dago who was dedicated to him. Those of us who have been in that situation have heard those lies time and time again. Some women actually use their brains and leave. I just kept on wishing upon a star, reading books about creating a life via attraction principles, and staying true. I think I'm one of those girls who stays too long at the fair.

His mother, the matriarch of the entire family, passed away a month before we met. You realize that Italian boys and their mamas are inseparable, and I tried to sympathize with his grief, giving him a free pass to lie. She was an icon of Legend Music, working hard alongside Ron until the day she passed. Shortly after, his brother passed. Then his son. All within a year and a half.

Unfortunately, there was another kind of death happening that blind-sided him as much as the others. I grew weary of being his little sex kitten playing "You Can Leave Your Hat On" games. My big act was when we were at a club. I would have the band play the song. I would bring a chair out to the center of the dance floor and work my magic for all the world to see. It was over-the-top, fifty shades of sexy, and he loved it, as did his business associates.

It's exciting to run and hide and meet at seedy bars in the middle of the day—for a brief window of time, very brief. Eventually, the little meetings got boring and added to the feeling of my resentment and anger when he was in Orlando or Italy with his family. I grew quiet and sullen. I remember the words of Frankie, warning me of what could happen. Eventually, mostly from public embarrassment, I tried to break up with him or pretended to break it off. Still weak, I allowed him to persuade me to stay. Again, he started with the lies about leaving after another major event in his life or his kids'. This went on for years. I heard time and time again "I will leave."

I guess I turned into a total bitch. I know why there are so many songs about romantic relationships. Love is truly a magnificent mystery. We know when we're in it, and we definitely know when we're not. I asked Ron once why he lived such a double life, keeping all of us separated like chess pieces. He remarked arrogantly, "Because I can." I pushed for more explanations many times, and he must have thought it was cheeky to reply, "I've sold my soul to Faust." What? Hello? I'm the church girl, remember. Could Kabbalah be true, that equal amounts of energy are drawn to each other? The greater the light, the greater the darkness it draws.

Tired of the lying, hiding, sneaking, I took Dana and Grant to Florida between the time his brother and son died. Dana went to the University of Miami, and Grant went to high school where I was a language arts teacher in Coral Springs.

Almost three years later, my mom finally told us she was terminally ill. I never realized what a private person she was. I returned to Youngstown and took a consultant position with a mental health facility and took a chance once again on Ron. Old habits die hard. And once again, he swore that he would leave after his daughter's high school graduation. After the party, he came over and arrogantly dropped the ball, sitting on my floor with his sunglasses in his hands, "It's just not a good time." The look in my eye must have been murderous, and he brought out the big guns to keep me attached to him. It was in plain, crappy terms, a bribe to stay connected to me. I guess he loved me in some strange way. He gave me the keys to an actual mini-mansion hidden behind the wall of a very secluded resort community in South Florida. I took the bait. The house was amazing, and when I awoke there were people to clean the pool, landscape the yard, and guard the castle walls. It was decorated by high-end decorators with the best of the best, and I loved it. This was nothing a single guidance counselor with two kids could ever afford on her own. There, I admit it: I caved for the lifestyle, and he wasn't even going to be there. He flew back to be with the wife, and one thing was different; I wasn't crying, losing sleep, or worrying about what he was up to anymore. In fact, on the contrary, I figured that a little distance was good. I could handle him in Ohio. I pretended that I didn't care where he lived. I masqueraded that I was hard and healthy and done with him. But the outside isn't where it counts, and what's hiding on the inside will always find its way up and out of the deception we tell ourselves. On the inside, I still loved him, flaws and all.

While in Florida, I never met anyone, nor did I sleep with anyone. I only sleep with a man whom I love deeply. No one-night stands for me. I've just never been into that.

I lived in Florida with my kids for four years, learning about the real world outside Youngstown, Ohio. A slow but strangely empowering transformation occurred inside me that I wasn't even aware of until I went back to Ohio. I found interests I liked, people to socialize with, and I liked who I was becoming. I had finally had the courage to step out of my own way to see who else I was hiding under this skin, and I liked her. On the flip side, I guess Ron's wife got tired of him cheating on her with me and his other girlfriends. They finally did get a divorce. I guess you could say I was shocked. I was thinking I'd just coast until I met someone new. I was content to be alone. The quiet and the water are healing for me. In fact, I don't need a lot of people around me. I much prefer a few people I'm intimate with than crowds, which is totally different than performing. Stage life is not real life; I learned that about myself in South Florida.

Although I missed Ron, my focus was my job and my kids, and the truth is, life goes on and people begin to find a life wherever they are. Dana was graduating from the University of Miami, and I had a lot of things to keep me busy. I studied angels, astrology, and tarot. I did yoga, walked, hung out in South Beach with my daughter, and took good care of myself. I even taught Sunday school.

I practiced for years, running the failures of my marriage like a bad movie that was on every channel, what a good wife I would be when and if I ever got another chance. I was going to get it right. Finally Ron was going to be free, and it was my opportunity to model for my children what a happy family looks like. But until now, those were only fantasies that I quite actually thought would stay there out somewhere in the universe as a dream. The horse is out of the gate, and I get the call: the divorce is final and "get your ass up here fast" comes through loud and clear. "I can't make it up here without you," he frantically ranted, obviously disappointed that I was preoccupied, finishing a small role in a play in Stuart, and couldn't return for another week.

I let this very real sign slip, trying to remember how devastating divorces were for everyone. I've got to conclude, though, after endless calls that this guy was clueless. He stayed at their home until the ink was dry and had made no plans for his future. I learned when I arrived that I was called upon to create his new world and his happily ever after because he thought I was the best candidate, not because he loved me. He is a man that cannot be without a woman. He needs a body. I hoped I was more than that, but I wasn't. To say the beginning of our life together was a total nightmare would be an understatement. I had given up a job as the dean of the guidance department in Port St. Lucie schools to start a life with the type of man I had dreamed of since I was a little girl, only to find my heart broken again. I was so excited when I got off that plane. We were going to get the keys to our first place, and with that came lots of decorating. It was modest, but we were in transition. When I fell for Ron, it was never about the money. It might have been his persona, energy, vitality, and kick-ass attitude, but it wasn't about the money. I considered that just the icing on the cake, though it was the best icing I've ever had the pleasure of sharing. He lived very well in comparison to my "save all week to go out on Saturday" teacher salary.

My world started to unravel just hours after I landed in Pittsburgh. There I was in Target, purchasing cleaning supplies, sheets, pillows, and blankets, when a little redheaded preteen, grinning from ear to ear like she saw Santa, came up to Ron while we waited in the checkout line. She says, "Hi, Ron. I just wanted to thank you for the guitar." I'm sure she was coached, as her single, thirtysomething mom stood a few aisles over, glaring at Ron. He got that stupid look of disbelief on his face. Why are guys always shocked as shit when they get cold busted? Dumb asses, seriously! The girl followed us out into the parking lot and stood in the middle of the road. Once again, I grew dead quiet. At the apartment, I busied myself creating what was to be our love nest.

The following evening Ron came home and was stark white. He told me he was seeing this girl and it was my fault because I was working in South Florida. Ron usually screams and denies everything, so trust me when I tell you this was at least a step in the right direction. However, he probably didn't have a choice. That girl was coming for me, end of story. I sat looking at the bare walls, without furniture, without the picture I planned for ten years of what my life would be when Ron and I finally could come out of hiding and be an actual couple. He promised me it was over. But he promised me he was going to leave his wife every other season for the last decade. I sat there in shock. All I could think of was Debbie, my New York spitfire, and the words "What did you expect!"

The next morning I received a call from our super, who said a woman and a child came in to deliver some things to me. I knew exactly whom she was referring to. When I arrived, the glamorous, buxom super said, "Honey, if that's Ron's other girlfriend, you have nothing to worry about." She handed me a bag full of letters, a stuffed animal, cards, men's sweaters, men's T-shirts, and men's underwear. I stoically walked back to our apartment and put the items in the trash without reading them. I phoned Ron.

So the first year of living in this little apartment was hell, pure hell. I tried everything to cook the right foods. I gained ten pounds. I often heard rude comments that the chicken was too tough or the spaghetti was too sweet or the courses were not heated properly.

Remember, I am a career woman with two degrees and had not been married for a long time. I gave up my high heels, business suits, and power attitude to relax and become the

Italian wife I thought this man wanted. I failed on every level. Nothing pleased him.

We toughed it out in Youngstown for a while, which was brutal. I often looked at other women and wondered if Ron had slept with them. I hated that I thought that way, but how could I avoid it with his reputation? I found out later that while I lived in his home in Florida, Ron was a busy boy, making deals both in and out of bed.

Ron impulsively decided to close his music store to semi-retire to Florida, and I was ecstatic. We hired people, and I worked right beside him so that the closeout was a very profit-able extravaganza. The day of the closing sale, this same girl who left clothes at our apartments barged in with the help of one of his dago buddies. She brought in a birthday cake and all the fixings. Dressed in my little NY Music T-shirt, I quiet-ly asked her not to do this. She pushed her hefty Midwestern self past me and went straight toward his office like a bull. It became a shit show. He was frozen in fear. I was momentarily insane. I couldn't quite make out the words coming out of her mouth. My mind clouded in chaos. Oh, she was pledging her love for him. I pushed her, and her cheap sunglasses flew under his desk. I regained some kind of composure, picked them up, and returned them her. She said how old I looked! I freaked out again. She picked up her glasses, turned, and kissed him, wishing him a happy birthday. He stood there like the snake he is, searching for the nearest rock to climb back under.

I stormed out of the store. I called my aunt. She helped settle my nerves and directed me to go back into that store and work the sale. I did. But right there, I was done. Something died in me that morning. Something that is missing that all the gifts, shopping trips, and cars cannot remove. The bleeding increased, leaving stains now seen on my physical countenance.

We finally moved back to Tesoro, to my small castle in South Florida. The warm, salty air and balmy nights revitalized my high hope that we might just make it as a couple. I lost those dreaded ten pounds, got my Lilly Pulitzer pinks on, and felt like April Gatta again. I felt that Florida was my home, and I wanted it to be Ron's home too. I introduced him to people in groups that were important to me. He tried but still couldn't move on. His feet were in Youngstown, where everyone knew him, worshipped him, and did his bidding. I'm not sure how someone so successful wouldn't be thrilled to live the good life, but he was miserable. I guess driving a brand-new, loaded Mercedes in a neighborhood where it's just an OK car wasn't what he needed. I felt comfortable; he felt something less than that. I'm from no money, but I've worked hard and feel very relaxed in groups with diverse backgrounds. In fact, I find it revitalizing to learn so much from others. They give me gifts of stories of lives I have not lived, and I am openly grateful for their friendship.

I believe that happiness happens at the moment wherever you are with the ones you love. I also had two children who needed to be embraced by his arms and his protection.

It took a few years, but Ron eventually did embrace Dana. So much so he paid for her wedding and walked her down the aisle by the Hudson River at the Rhinecliff Hotel. However, that wedding was one time that I let him put me through hell for the sake of someone I loved more than life itself. To cut costs, I became the wedding planner, the florist, the maid of honor, the one who gave the showers, doing it one step at a time, one trip to Hobby Lobby at a time, one order from a wholesale company at a time. It became a very long process, although I enjoyed doing it. It's just sad that he took a lot of fun out of it, especially on the day of the rehearsal dinner. He said loudly to Dana and me, "I want you to write down the entire cost of this wedding right now." Dana ran out to do some yoga moves, and I glared at him like a shark. The same shark eyes he gave to me for so many years.

I wasn't always a shark. One year at Christmas, I sat in a corner in a bustier, thong, and garters, wrapped in twinkling lights like an elf, waiting for him to come home. When he burst through the door, his first words were, "Is dinner ready?"

Why should I bother? I unwrapped myself alone in our bedroom. I don't remember what I fixed for dinner. I was too hurt to care or remember.

That kind of thing tore me apart, as well as vicious comments such as "no one would ever want you," "no one would put up with you but me," "nobody gets you because they think you're weird," "you're odd," or "you're getting old." Every woman, every spiritual woman, every beautiful woman hates to hear those things.

I tried my very best to please him, so he bought a stunning home on the lake to spend eight months out of the year at home in Youngstown. I returned a little concerned about his floundering ways with women, but he made me an offer I couldn't refuse. We split our time, and I get to go back to Tesoro each winter. Youngstown is a place like none other, and of course my stepdad, my biological dad, and my son, Grantster, were there. The people there are unique to say the least, indescribable, one of a kind. I quickly realized that my upscale decorating didn't please Ron. He and his friends ridiculed me for the choices I made in colors and furniture, though I scoured the stores for deals. Yes, I had definitely changed while I was living away. My Tesoro friends told me to ignore them and keep doing what I do. One very respected and highly educated lady, Margot, scolded me, "Be strong. Take a stand about your life, and don't put up with anything that degrades you. Never run, and live your life right where you are." That is more difficult than it seems. How can you push through when the one you love criticizes your choices over and over? Each snide comment is a pinprick in the heart, causing more blood loss.

In the summer, we went to couple's counseling. Ron went twice. I went all summer. I had told him about my lovely lady friends in Tesoro. He kindly responded, "Some women can turn their heads and live quietly, playing the game. I'm not sure you are one of those women." I nearly had a nervous breakdown after that first summer of putting together our first home. I had no money, no job, and no hope that he would ever really like the person I had become. When someone picks apart every little thing you do, with words and tone, it takes a toll mentally. It's tough to have a healthy sense of self-esteem and pride.

As the Jewish mobster says in *The Godfather* at his birthday in Havana, talking to Michael about the assignation of Moe Green, "This is the life I chose." As you can probably tell, I don't give up easily. I tried and tried again, because I made the commitment that this was the last for me. I wanted to see it through, and I have. Ron and I, at the time of writing this book, have been together for almost fifteen years.

Many women would have thrown in the towel. Not me. I'm not sure if I do that out of stupidity, being a hardheaded Italian, or because I truly love the men I make a commitment to.

Also, we had a history together. As the years rolled on, I aged. That's not something I could control. We all age. I felt less confident about myself. My children grew up. I couldn't escape into their activities, their plans, their hopes. Grant drifted away from me, for many reasons. I love Grant but have realized now that he is an adult, that I was afraid of making a mistake while raising him. I wasn't sure of how to raise a boy by myself. I shouldn't have pulled away. That decision has had ramifications deep into Grant's adult life.

For the last few years, I have been miserable. Was it really

Ron's fault? No. I hold myself responsible for everything that I have put my heart, my children, and my family through. Throughout all the years, I must admit we have become very, very good friends. I've tried to help him, with counseling, spirituality, couples' groups, walks, talks, meditation, and yoga. I reached out to give him more of what I thought would open up his heart. I've learned an important lesson: those are do-it-yourself jobs, and no one can do the deep, dark work for someone else.

It may sound like I really don't love Ron. I do. But again, I found myself in a relationship that I should never have entered. It may seem that Ron has been the meanest, most awful guy in the world. He's not. He's a first-generation Italian who thinks and lives simply. "Live by the gun, die by the gun" mentality. They don't trust politicians, doctors, or lawyers. His motto is "Everyone has a use. Take them for who they are, and get what you can to make your own life work." His life has changed drastically recently, and I've stuck with him for a reason. He has provided in many ways. He cares as much as he's capable.

Ron is adorable and cunning, and when he is at his best, a lot of women would gladly get in line for a piece of him. Many people are attracted to snake charmers. I know now that I fell for Ron for the wrong reasons again. And for that, I'm eternally sorry that I picked him as a substitute for someone else. Even if a person is totally shallow, they don't deserve to be a second-choice or a good-enough mate. We all seem to arrive at love's door with secret little agendas, kept from our partners and perhaps ourselves, until the lies drop and we're sitting at the bottom of the hill with a bucket of rotten apples on our heads. Each person deserves someone who cherishes them for being "the one," not close to "the one."

CHAPTER 9

Big Girls Do Cry

Imprinting 101

Imprinting is a dysfunctional thought impairment linked to inaccurate early beliefs about love and romance formed during a specific developmental window of time during childhood. I believe that most mental health issues, like addictions, never completely vanish but can be successfully managed through therapy, education, and self-determination. Knowledge about the disorder and assistance utilizing appropriate techniques can avoid falling prey to triggers and eventual relapse.

For example, let's share some insights about addiction. Regardless of age or background, there is always a risk of relapse. Even after all the work we do, it's a slippery slope to maintain those healthy thoughts of hope for all our dreams to come shining through. Overcoming this addiction is a lifetime commitment made one moment at a time, a day at a time, one temptation at a time. Within the parameters of addiction, each individual must learn from what, with whom, and when their weakness slips and they are about to fall for the wrong person once again. Is imprinting in the DSM-5 as a real mental illness? No, but maybe it should be.

Because few openly discuss and work with issues of imprinting, I am part of the multi-generational repeating cycle, mostly from ignorance or denial to look at ourselves in the bleak sunlight of truth. This disability has no gender bias. Both men and women often fall for the same type of partner over and over and over until they wake up and realize something isn't right. In fact, something is desperately wrong. My imprinting burned a deep hole in my love life that I would never permit anyone to fill but Frankie. Every man, hell, every possible suitor, was measured against the one who imprinted on me—Frankie Valli.

Please don't think that I'm asking you to jump on the bandwagon and burn Mr. Valli at the stake, though I'm sure he has had a part in this heartache of mine. I'm still very protective of him, though I'm sure some may judge it quite differently because I'm even writing about him. What's so mysterious about love? We all have a love story inside us that screams to come out. The haters will hate, the players will play, and the lovers, the dreamers, and I will want to be imprisoned until we let it out, share it with others.

Part of me still loves him because I understand him, where he came from, and the state of his life during those years. Frankie was a megastar who was surrounded by a team of people who allowed him his every wish. That kind of treatment has to affect a person. Let's face it: power is the greatest aphrodisiac for humans. He had throngs of fans who fell asleep listening to his songs on the radio every night and dreamed of being in his arms. He didn't come from money, so I assume this newfound elaborate lifestyle was shocking and took time to adjust to and fathom. Rising to fame in the era of the sexual revolution and experimentation with drugs made his risky behaviors seem quite normal for a man of his stature. Frankie Valli had more hits, more power, and more ego than he knew what to do with.

If a non-celebrity was given the free rein Frankie has with women, they would satisfy their urges and fantasies, pushing the envelope whenever they could.

I also believe from my experiences with Frankie that he was not a highly educated man and was led mostly by impulse and ego. Frankie has had his bouts with cocaine addiction, anorexia, womanizing, and family feuds, as the cost of fame is quite steep. That said, I don't believe Frankie was grooming me in any way, had thought he was hurting me, or thought much at all about me and his effect on my life and my heart.

My soul chants to me that this is what was supposed to happen, when it happened, how it happened. That all is in perfection because Frankie and I have some sort of pre-agreement, and there is, in fact, a predestined karmic connection between us. Something that we revisited many times, unaware of our souls' intentions. I love him. I always will. I did the imprinting. He was my idol, my ideal, my one and only. I certainly don't love him like I did when I was a child. How can I not love someone whom I first fell in love with when I was a child? When I fell in love with him, he became my imprinter.

Looking back now at a distance and as more of an observer of my life, I see Mr. Valli innocent in most of what occurred to me on a psychological level. Mr. Valli is a megastar with endless amounts of power. Power, if not reined in with wisdom, leads to a life dominated by immediate gratification, driven by ego. His bout with anorexia and binge eating amounts of maple syrup indicates control issues, difficulties with accepting aging, and a desire to stay on top of his game.

In the spring of 2014, I read with the rest of the world

the lawsuit that Frankie won against his ex-wife about life insurance money. Most couples fight over money, so I didn't think much about it. It was the Fourth of July, and my family and I were texting each other from Ohio to New York to Chicago about Frankie Valli performing at the White House. He looked handsome. He performed wonderfully, sounding better than ever.

The next morning, I received some news that startled me more than it should have. Randy Valli, Frankie's ex, died on July 4, 2014. Even though we never met, I was lost for a second, floating as though in a dream state of disbelief. My first thought was that I must not have heard correctly. My Frankie, of course, would not be out singing while his boys were helping their mother pass. Then as I came back to reality, I began to put the pieces of the lawsuit and the dates together. Shocked again, I thought it all can't be right, he would never take Randy to court, knowing she had leukemia. Would he? How could he? Who is this man? I admit I no longer know him. He's not the man I loved. I'm not sure that man ever existed!

Those of us who do manage to survive the rigors of life's lessons learn somehow to cry and carry on. I cry a lot. Maybe I cry too much for those uncomfortable sitting with truth. I feel sometimes that my lust for understanding makes others jittery. I see them pull back as the sting of their lessons sometimes melts into mine. I understand because it takes great courage to admit to sadness and disappointment openly. My generation was raised in a bubble where all our wants were presented to us at light speed. We all received blue ribbons just for showing up. We were taught that we were fabulous just because. On some level, I agree with that. But without the spiritual cornerstone of universal laws to add some sort of justice for both the positive and negative behaviors, there are a lot of antisocial, narcissistic adults who have raised more of the

same. I would rather stop, sit, and cry, and gather some peace
from an emotional collision crash. I always carry with me my
children's vision of my tea set with my dearest companions
sharing a cup of tea, looking out at the sky of grey, passing
the Kleenex as we assure one another that the sun will indeed
come out again

It's never easy when you are rejected. It conjures up every
rejection and every fear that we've had since we were born,
even the imaginary ones. The one you had when Dad left
Mom and you take on the belief that it was somehow your
fault. The first time friends left you out of a sleepover. We all
have those things happen to us. And as children, our percep-
tions often vary greatly from the actual truth. The pain in the
pit of your stomach is still very much a feeling of realizing,
"Oh no, another person left me. Why? Am I so hard to love?
What did I do to make everyone go? I'm such a loser. I'm not
good enough to deserve real love. I am utterly alone."

How foolishly arrogant I have been to think I could change
anyone. I've taken off my rose-colored glasses to realize it is
neither my right nor my duty to be a self-imposed guidance
counselor to anyone. Did you know that most people never
return after their first or second session in counseling and
that most feel better on their own in the time it would have
taken to complete twelve sessions? It is I and I only who is
responsible for myself. If on the way I can possibly send out
only positive, unconditional regard for someone else, yes, even
the men who hurt me most, perhaps that is truly a successful
life. The other route of playing goddess, healing the misguided
didn't work for me. Ron's beautiful daughter has reached out
as well, sharing similar stories about her mom. I have stopped
driving myself crazy trying to show Mr. Ron a better way. Is it
not his right to choose to believe or not? I have learned a valuable lesson from him. Row your boat gently down the stream,
as the children's nursery rhyme goes. I am no longer rowing

his boat. His boat has a leak in the center, and no matter how much water I get out, my bucket cannot get the job done.

The leak in Ron's boat has turned into a jagged hole. I used to laugh at this funny and very private story. It seems like years ago now, but Ron and I were making love in my tiny apartment when his little, fragile foot started to thump like a bunny. My precious nightmare Mr. Ron the music man and Youngstown's bag of chips, as we have appropriately named him, jumped up and freaked. He was tweaking, and he hit my nightstand, and my little jar of Billy's ashes flew all over the bed. That's the only threesome he will ever get, unless you count our Yorkie, Miss Roxie.

Today we spend most of our days going to doctors and considering options. I am just his girlfriend, and he will never marry me. I have no source of income, and I know I have choices, but none seems like the right one with the man I care for, or for the life I claim to be mine that still wants to grow and discover. I feel trapped like a mouse in a cage.

This spitfire playboy, power-hungry millionaire asks me to button his shirt, write a check, drive him to dinner. At one time he was so cruel and thoughtless about my feelings, and that still peeks through on his good days. The many personality side effects of Parkinson's include fear and depression. As I see Ron, I realize that his need for control has always been fueled but intense feelings of fear and paranoia. Now we are all in for a hell of a ride. When you give these feelings to someone who has always been a control freak, it's ugly and frustrating. It's odd, when someone gets sick, all the masks they have worn glued to their face fall to the ground. My precious nightmare is now sweeter than I could have ever imagined, and his mental issues are out there for the world to see, a side of him that he concealed from even those closest to him. We got an emotional therapy tag for our Yorkie, Roxie so she can travel with us everywhere. Now Ron spends his day worrying who will leave me first, Roxie or him. My, how a year changes things.

Is there a destiny that we are meant to have in this life? Or is life a series of crazy roller coaster rides to teach us lessons of self-love, self-forgiveness, and self-worth? We could be deluding ourselves, rationalizing our poor mistakes, thinking that it makes sense when it may all mean nothing. Some people like Ron are what I call runners. They go from one thing to the next to avoid asking themselves these very important questions. The result is a life cut short by disease on some level that will usually manifest somewhere in the physical body in the future. The result is that you limit yourself from crying and releasing the pain, the toxins, the agony to make room for what you truly want.

Sitting on my back porch, Roxie beside me, with my favorite book, *Journey of the Soul*, I'm tempted to recite a few lines to Ronnie. I bite my tongue, turning inward to hear my breathing and draw me back to my center. My affair with palm trees and sandhill cranes fill my life with joy, but I know this too will not last. Nothing ever does. I take sip of my green tea and hear, "Presh, did we have a doctor's appointment today?"

"No, presh, it's OK. I'm waiting on you to take a walk with me."

But there were clouds coming. Ron wanted to move back to Youngstown permanently. His condition declined more rapidly than we had anticipated. His lapse in memory caused constant questions about everything. He would say, "Do we have enough food?" "I feel like I'm in a coffin," "I hate this house," "I have no one," "You don't take care of me." He wanted to be at home, and I couldn't blame him. It wasn't the disease that bothered me, however; it was his mental issues. And for me, it meant no more Florida, no more dancing, no more laughter, not even a marriage proposal, only another trap. He agreed that I would have some financial reward upon his death if I behaved and did what he wanted; after all, he reminded me, "That's what you get your allowance for."

On a snowy day when I was finally going to get out of the house, Ron scolded, "I don't want someone who gets her hair and nails done. I want someone who just stays home and takes care of me." Once again, I was shaken from my core. I had given up the gym and seeing my daughter in New York (he hates the city and refuses to go and now can't be alone due to his fears). I left Florida in February, in the coldest season ever. I dosed off and on, staring at the television screen, watching snow storms and subzero temperatures with Roxie, dressed in my pj's, munching on pretzel sticks, searching for answers. All I could do was pray. I searched to find out how to get back to the lady who laughed and danced and awaited each new day with joy.

Dear God,

I realize and integrate into the deepest parts of you that no one sees these thoughts of Ron, Marc, Billy, or Frankie. I realize that relationships come and go for the highest growth in everyone concerned.

To each of them I humbly pray:

I am grateful for you.
I set you free to do what you have to do.
I love that we touched and were in each other's space.
Be free.
Let us all be free.

Thank you.

The odd thing about healing is that when you forgive someone, you become free, lighter, and forgiven. By the way, none of us are perfect, and we have to look at our role in why the relationship didn't last.

I once knew a young woman who met a man who was in med school. They dated for several months. As they were making love one night, he noticed a bump and told her to get it checked out. It was cancer. He broke up with her shortly after, admitting he wasn't up to dealing with this kind of issue in a relationship.

At first, that seems heartless and cold. On the other hand, you could say he saved her life. If she had been single and not been intimate with anyone, she might not have noticed the lump. Perhaps his brief time with her was his soul's purpose for this encounter.

Healing is not easy if it occurs at all. I 1,000 percent know in my heart that it will arrive to a place in each of us at the perfect time, but I've also experienced and witnessed that the kind of transformation I'm referring to doesn't usually arrive in one quick kneeling at the altar, though I'm not diminishing the profound effect a spiritual awakening can have in holy instant in the quiet space of spirit's presence. The real stuff inside, the self-loathing, the multi-generational messages, the early memories, and memories of previous lives take time, sometimes months or even lifetimes to expose, discover, and dissolve within our souls, freeing us to remember who we are. We are perfect, safe, loved, and eternal. Each person has free will that allows each of us to create the lesson they learn and when they learn it. When you're ready to heal, here are some steps that I have found helpful in my life. Say them out loud if necessary. In some cases, you might need to do these steps multiple times. That's OK. Whatever works best for you.

1. I, [insert your name here], give myself permission for the feelings to come out, no matter how silly they may appear.

2. I tune in to what my heart is telling me, what my body is doing. (It's a consciousness very similar to meditation.)

3. If my mind is tired, I don't read. If my legs are weary, I sit. If my soul is tired, I enjoy something simple, like watching birds. If I am drained, I withdraw and sleep. (I've done a lot of that lately, and I know I have more healing to do. I don't force myself to be someone I'm not right now. There will be more parties, more laughter, more sunny days.)

4. I will stand back as an observer and objectively try to look at my life through an unbiased lens.

5. After enough of the rage has left, I will try to see the positive aspects. (Don't kid yourself, though, the rage will return. Then say, "What have I learned? How have I grown?")

From this list, ponder how to make something positive out of this. For me, I have written this book, and as a counselor, I present the idea of imprinting and how it might have affected others' love lives. I talk to a therapist and get a second opinion. Everyone needs someone to bounce ideas off of. Find a good one.

I get up in the morning and find myself a little stronger and ready to pull back the draperies and start again. I know one thing: I still hear a small voice that keeps saying, "April Lynn, you're not done yet." This voice sustains me. I am here to work. It will find me. I will find it.

It would be impossible to discuss romance and love without including spirituality. Love is the source of all healing, and through our lovers, this sacred space is opened for our growth and evolution.

I hope the steps you have just read in this chapter will help you recover and heal. Again, don't kid yourself that it will be easy. If your recovery is easy, you probably didn't have much invested in the relationship anyway.

But if you are like me, you have invested a lot into your current relationship, or the one that you need help recovering from. In either case, the healing will come. Give it time. There is truth in the saying, time does heal all wounds. Also put some effort into your healing. Anything worth having in life takes effort and energy. That includes healing from a broken heart.

If we could clearly define imprinting as an actual disorder, we could offer people hope. They could finally get off the merry-go-round of drama and loss in love. As a disorder, imprinting could offer a list of symptoms, effects, and possible causes. In addition, therapeutic options and recovery methods would give those whose heart has been broken a light at the end of the tunnel. Those who are afflicted will see that it's not their fault. Programs would be developed with support groups offering counseling for all who have been affected. Parenting classes for early interventions would prevent this syndrome from becoming a generational condition. If we were aware of imprinting, that pivotal developmental stage could create dialogue thwarting later issues. In short terms, the more each of us understand romantic love and passion, the more each of us will have a chance to find the kind of relationship we all want and deserve. Creating a platform for such dialogue would also prohibit getting misdiagnosed, labeled with terms that can sometimes seem too vague. Terms like "situational depression" or "adjustment disorder." These terms are only Band-Aids allowing us legal methods of self-medicating and a socially appropriate explanation to others for our major screw ups as well as easing our own bruised egos. During which we continue the exhausting pursuit of finding love in all of the wrong places, as our children imitate and recreate the behavior of which we could have changed had we'd been given the tools.